WAR!

*It is fear and suffering and
death and earsplitting violence.*

*Our battalion fought as often and as well
as any other combat unit in Vietnam. . . .
Traditionally, the place of the battalion
chaplain was at the aid station with the
surgeon, where he could give solace to the
wounded and dying. But Vietnam is a different
war. . . .*

ABOUT THE AUTHOR

Chaplain (Major) James M. Hutchens is a graduate of Wheaton College (Ill.) and Dallas Theological Seminary. He went to Vietnam as Chaplain with the 70th Engineer Battalion and then transferred to the combat tested 173d Airborne Brigade. Major Hutchens is holder of the Bronze Star medal for heroism and the Purple Heart. He is now assigned to the 6th Special Forces Group (The Green Berets) at Ft. Bragg, N.C.

BEYOND COMBAT

JAMES M. HUTCHENS
Chaplain (Major) US Army

Foreword by
Major General Ellis W. Williamson

MOODY PRESS • CHICAGO

DEDICATED
To all my men, for to be
trusted is even
greater than to be loved

BEYOND COMBAT

A MOODY PRESS BOOK
Published by Pyramid Publications for Moody Press

Paperback edition published April 1970
   Second printing, January 1972

Library of Congress Catalog Card Number: 68-31200

Printed in the United States of America

MOODY PRESS BOOKS are published by Moody Press
820 North LaSalle Street, Chicago, Illinois 60610, U.S.A.

Contents

Photo section follows page 64

CHINA

NORTH VIETNAM

CHINA

• Hanoi
Haiphong

LAOS

GULF
OF
TONKIN

AN KHE—base camp of the
70th Engineer Battalion
BIEN HOA—home of the 173d
Airborne Brigade

17th Parallel

Hue

THAILAND

SOUTH

• Dak To
• Kontum
Pleiku
19 An Khe
Deo Mang Pass Qui Nhon

CENTRAL
HIGHLANDS

CAMBODIA

VIETNAM

GULF
OF
SIAM

Hill 65
Bien Hoa

Saigon

MEKONG
DELTA

SOUTH CHINA SEA

Foreword

I have seen the American fighting man under many stresses in three great military conflicts of this century. From the Normandy landings in Europe to the Inchon invasions in Korea, and more recently in army ground combat unit action in Vietnam, my responsibilities in the armed forces, coupled with the fact that I was raised in a devoutly religious home of seven children, have exposed me to a broad spectrum of man and his approach to God.

This excellent book covers matters of life and death in a manner I haven't seen in writing. It exposes a view of war and man himself in such a way that the reader will find himself growing stronger in spirit. Each individual mentioned and each incident is real to me, for I was there. But I'm sure each reader will feel that he has been there too, participating in these experiences. He will see that in war no man stands alone.

Combat experiences—especially when the outcome is in doubt—do something to a man. Pomposity and grandeur are swept away, exposing him as he really is. Difficult combat also dissolves feelings of selfishness. The soldier, almost without knowing it, becomes a highly motivated component of the group. In these times a man knows himself better, too. His true values become important, overshadowing shortcomings and disappointments. The man emerges proud of himself, able to understand more than he previously could about his approach to these values.

Combat is a horrible experience. No commander that is close to it could ever enjoy it. However, all is not on the negative side. A man who has faced death, faced his God and lived properly with his fellow soldiers comes out of combat experience a better man.

Chaplain Hutchens has done an excellent job of putting down in this book the vivid accounts of men living and dying in the discipline of war. I consider it a privilege and indeed a pleasure to prepare the Foreword for *Beyond Combat*.

Ellis W. Williamson
Major General, US Army

Acknowledgments

To all who have made the completion of this book possible, my deepest thanks. Of the many chaplains who gave encouragement and direction, I want to especially thank Chaplain (Colonel) Chester R. Lindsey, Deputy Chaplain U.S. Conarc, for his keen spiritual perceptivity in evaluating portions of the manuscript, and Chaplain (Lieutenant Colonel) Burton G. Hatch, my spiritual father who many years back was a faithful Paul to a fledgling Timothy.

To Colonel Samuel V. Wilson, Commanding Officer, 6th Special Forces Group (Airborne) 1st Special Forces, and Captain Ben W. Lagare, a fellow soldier from the 173d Airborne Brigade (Separate), for proofreading the final manuscript. I am indebted to Lieutenant Colonel James Anderson, my executive officer in 1st Battalion (Airborne) 503d Infantry of the 173d Airborne Brigade (Separate), and to Chaplain (Major) Virgil Cooley, group chaplain of the 7th Special Forces Group (Airborne) 1st Special Forces, who provided some of the photographs included. Materials from the John F. Kennedy Center for Special Warfare Library at Fort Bragg, North Carolina, were used in formulating chapter 3.

I am particularly grateful to my sister-in-law, Miss

Wanda Ann Mercer, for her advice and technical assistance, and to Norman B. Rohrer for professional competence rendered in preparing the final manuscript for publication.

Certainly a special note of gratitude goes to my wife, Patty, who typed the manuscript and made many valuable suggestions. Her deep spiritual insight, her encouragement and prayers, constantly fanned the coals of waning spirit.

Most important of all, I render thanks to the Captain of my salvation, whose promises are new each day to him who believes.

1

The Deo Mang Pass

Sergeant (E-8) Delaneous Gossett was First Sergeant of Bravo Company—a mountain of a man with hands like anvils and a voice like sandpaper. He was long on courage too, but for all the confidence his hulking six-foot, six-inch frame and 260-pound body exuded, he was fully aware of the dangers we were about to face.

"Well, Chaplain," he boomed, "this is going to be a long stretch of Indian territory. Next time you're looking up, say one for me."

"I'll do that, Sergeant," I promised, "but I'm sure He would like it a lot better direct from you. Nothing like OJT (on-the-job training), you know."

"Top" smiled as he crammed himself into his jeep. He started the engine and began to move out.

The jagged bluffs and vine-covered arroyos of the Vietnam "Indian country" made the Deo Mang Pass an ideal ambush site. The senior soldiers of Bravo Company agreed that if the Viet Cong were going to hit our convoy, this would be the place. Veterans of World War II and the Korean conflict had started early to pass out the "hot skinny" from "Rumor Con-

trol." As soon as word got out that we would negotiate the Deo Mang Pass, war stories began circu-
lating, growing more intense with each retelling. By
the time they filtered down to the green young pri-
vates they bore tinges of all-out nuclear offensive by
"Charlie," our crafty enemy of the jungle.

Still, the thought of subjecting ourselves to the
enemy in the narrow pass seemed ominous, and the
men gingerly cleaned and fondled their weapons. My
assistant had managed to acquire a couple of extra
magazines of ammunition for his M-14 rifle which he
propped up between the seats of our jeep—"just in
case."

Along the Deo Mang Pass on March 30, 1954, elements of the hard-nosed 803d Infantry Regiment of
the Vietnam Peoples Army, better known as the Viet
Minh or forerunners of the Viet Cong, annihilated an
infantry battalion of French Group Mobile Number
11. Would we be spared such a fate?

As we waited quietly for the signal to start, my assistant looked at me quizzically. "Well, sir, what do
you think?"

"I think we ought to commit ourselves and this trip
to the Lord and play it heads up all the way," I replied.

An alert hush fell on the entire company as we
bowed our heads and placed ourselves once again in
His hands.

At three o'clock in the morning the engines came to
life and we took our place in the motorized column on
the outskirts of Qui Nhon, our seaport bivouac area.
The strategy was to bring the remaining two companies plus battalion headquarters to the An Khe area,
the new home of the unit to which I was assigned—
the Army's 70th Engineer Battalion (Combat)
(Army).

Sporadic sniper fire from small arms punctuated

our move out of Qui Nhon, but no one was hit, and soon the monotonous drone of the four-cylinder jeep engine seemed to whisper calm assurance as we began the four-mile trek through the pass.

Back and forth—left and right—zigzagging on countless hairpin turns we climbed higher and higher, crawling like drugged turtles along precipitous fifty-degree slopes. Perched on those cliffs we were highly vulnerable targets for Viet Cong bullets as the French had been a decade and a year earlier.

The Deo Mang Pass guards the eastern entrance to Vietnam's Central Highland plateau country along Route 19. It slices through the mountains just ahead of the village of An Khe as one travels west from the seaport of Qui Nhon. Under electric-blue skies I had flown over the pass a week before by helicopter en route to An Khe to hold Sunday services for two of our companies already there. The pass was an awesome sight from the air, but creeping through it by convoy made it look even more ominous. Fortunately, our escort consisted of elements of the 1st Brigade of the crack 101st Airborne Division. They provided us with flank security by positioning their men along the route of march at bridges, crossroads, high ground, and at the bamboo and barbed wire walls that surrounded the many hamlets we passed through. "Gun jeeps" equipped with thirty-caliber machine guns mounted front and rear darted in and out of the convoy. They were a noisy but comforting spectacle.

As we crept steadily through the pass the events and circumstances that had brought me to this place began filling my mind and I lived them again in retrospect.

The 70th Engineer Battalion stationed at Fort Campbell, Kentucky, had been my first assignment on active duty as a chaplain. I had served there in 1955 and 1956 as an enlisted man in the 511th Airborne Infantry Regiment of the since deactivated 11th Airborne Division.

At Fort Campbell I had received Jesus Christ as my Savior, under the ministry of our regimental chaplain, Burton Hatch. I met Chaplain Hatch when I went down to our chapel one day with an old soldier who was trying to get out of the Army. This veteran of World War II and the Korean conflict was having domestic troubles and wanted to go home. On our way to one of the enlisted men's clubs we stopped to see if the chaplain could help him.

While my friend discussed his problems with one of the chaplains I waited in the vestibule inspecting the literature on display. Suddenly the door opened and the pleasant face of Chaplain Burton Hatch appeared, smiling a greeting. He paused a moment for a chat and then seated himself in a chair next to me because our conversation shifted to spiritual matters.

I had read the Bible some and was reared in a nominally Christian home. It was assumed that everybody "believed," but no one talked much about it. Later I had begun to question the basic underpinnings of Christianity. If God were indeed love, I wanted to know, why was there so much war, poverty and injustice in the world? How could Christ be a man and God at the same time? My biggest question had to do with miracles. What were they? Did they really occur? Why don't we see them today? How could the sea be parted—a man survive three days in the stomach of a great fish without being consumed by its digestive juices—the sun be moved back in its course? So the questions went.

Coupled with my questions was an awareness of my own purposelessness which at times overwhelmed me. A night out on the town with the boys left me even emptier than before. Beneath all this void was a kind of desperate hope that there was more to life than I was getting out of it, but it had never occurred to me that I was looking for it in the wrong direction.

Chaplain Hatch and I talked on and on there in the vestibule. I saw that this man had some answers. I quizzed him a bit on some of my deeper problems, and each time he gave me a sane, logical and biblical answer. Since it seemed I could learn a great deal from this chaplain I made an appointment to see him again.

That day I went back to my barracks, found a Bible and began to look for questions to stump the chaplain. When we met I fired my questions at him, each time receiving a satisfactory answer based on teaching from the same Book I had used to manufacture the problem.

Several months later my fuzzy view of the Scriptures suddenly snapped into focus.

"You know, Jim," Chaplain Hatch said, "we have been discussing spiritual things for some time now. We've talked about Jesus Christ and what He has done for us. Let me ask you this, Jim: Have you ever personally placed your faith in Christ?"

I picked up the key word and asked, "What do you mean by *faith?*"

The chaplain's reply was a startling unfolding of the foundation of truth.

"Jim," he said, taking a quarter from his pocket, "I'm going to give you this quarter. Do you believe me?"

"Yes, sir," I replied. "If you say you'll give it to me, I believe you will."

"But," he continued, "how can you know for sure I'll give it to you?"

"Well, I guess I would have to take your word for it, sir, and then reach out and take it."

"Then do it!" he told me.

As I reached out to take the quarter he grasped my hand in his and said softly, "Jim, that is the hand of *faith*."

Suddenly it all became clear. I could have sat there "believing" for a lifetime, but if I had never reached out and taken the quarter offered to me it would never have been mine. What had been so nebulous before finally began to take shape.

I heard Chaplain Hatch say, "Now let me ask you again, Jim. Have you ever placed your faith in Jesus Christ as your Savior?"

"No, I guess I haven't," I replied.

"Would you like to?"

"Yes, I would."

He suggested we bow in prayer and that I ask Jesus Christ to come into my heart and life. With a simple prayer I did just that, and nothing has been quite the same since that day.

Even here on the dangerous Deo Mang Pass things were different because of it. We took another hairpin curve, careful to maintain the interval between the two-and-a-half-ton truck in front of us. Then the road straightened out and my mind returned again to Fort Campbell and Chaplain Hatch and those wonderful days that followed.

A spiritual dimension had been added to my life. By a miracle, which I'll never fully understand, God invaded my life and became a reality to me through the person of the Lord Jesus Christ. The Bible became a new book because I began to understand its message. I read books Chaplain Hatch gave me which taught me basic truths of the Bible. Being linked to God through Christ affected every area of my life, supplying the meaning and purpose I had previously sought in vain.

After finishing my tour in the Army I attended Wheaton College and then Dallas Theological Seminary. A growing conviction told me God wanted me back in the military as a chaplain. Imagine my excitement when I was assigned to active duty as a chaplain in the United States Army! It seemed appropriate that I be returned to Fort Campbell to serve where my new life began. I was assigned to Chapel Eleven —the very place where I had made my initial commitment to Christ some nine years earlier.

Then things began happening fast. Less than two months after I returned to active duty there was a rapid military buildup following incidents at the Tonkin Gulf off Vietnam. Although the context of circumstances that constitute the "Tonkin Gulf Incident" is somewhat cloudy, certain facts are available. The official position of the United States maintains that on August 2, 1964, three North Vietnamese patrol boats engaged in an attack on American warships in the Tonkin Gulf. The American response to this through a Pentagon spokesman was that the situation was "unwelcome but not serious" (New York Times, August 3, 1964).

On August 4, 1964, however, a second attack was launched by an undetermined number of North Vietnamese PT boats on the United States destroyers "Maddox" and "C. Turner Joy." In response to this the United States launched heavy air attacks against three North Vietnamese coastal bases and, according to Secretary of Defense Robert McNamara, destroyed the bases along with twenty-five boats and demolished the local fuel depots.

While it would be an oversimplification to say that the "Tonkin Gulf Incident" produced the bloody engagement in Vietnam, it can certainly be truthfully stated that it served as a watershed for American precedent and policy in Southeast Asia.

That very month the 70th was alerted for a possible early deployment to a "critical area in Southeast Asia." We all knew where that was and planned accordingly.

Quickly our unit was brought up to full manpower strength. A series of records checks made sure every man had his personal business in order—proper family allotment, powers of attorney, wills, immunization shots including smallpox, yellow fever, cholera, tetanus, typhus, typhoid and others. Old equipment was repaired or replaced.

I began a series of Sunday sermons to prepare my men spiritually as well for our dangerous journey. I preached on such issues as our responsibility to our government (Romans 13), the sixth commandment ("Thou shalt not kill"), and the problem of the Christian serving in the Army. Also, I worked overtime helping the wives and families of the men in our unit.

When the readiness date came we were ready, eager to start. But no further orders were received. We remained on alert status. Days passed, then weeks, then months until the sands of nearly a full year had run through the glass. Then it happened!

Orders directed us to leave by plane on August 4, 1965, for San Francisco and thence by ship to that "critical area of Southeast Asia." Our equipment and baggage were sent by rail to the West Coast and on to Vietnam by ship, scheduled to arrive shortly ahead of us.

After the first few days of electrifying activity, the stark, solemn gravity of our situation began seeping into our minds. Like a jolt I realized that the discipline of war would tear me away from my beloved family. I would not be seeing them again for one year —maybe never again on this earth. How could we be certain of returning? We were involved in hot war with real bullets aimed by a well-trained, dedicated enemy. No man going to war can be sure he will come home—not even a chaplain.

Military life has a way of cementing strong family ties. One reason for this, I suppose, is that the military community is a society on the move. Since roots seldom go down deep in one spot, family members draw closer to each other. Often the religious, recreational and social lives of the military man are more family-centered than those of the civilian. A soldier's mobile home is indeed his "castle," and he is loath to leave it —even if he happens to be a chaplain. But the Lord and the Army call—frequently far from home.

Patty shared the strain of parting. So did Matt (three) and little Sarah (one and a half). When my orders came, Patty and I began preparing the children for my long absence.

"Daddy is going to take a boat trip across the ocean," we told them. "He will be away for a long time."

"What are you going to do?" Matt wanted to know.

"I'll be telling other soldiers about Jesus," I explained. That seemed to satisfy his little-boy curiosity.

We began also to make the coming year apart a specific matter for prayer. Foremost was the petition that God make the year spiritually profitable for each member of our family, a year that would count for all eternity. We prayed—almost desperately—that the Savior would be lifted up and that men would be drawn to Him.

How appropriate for us was God's promise to Isaiah: "And it shall come to pass, that before they call, I will answer; and while they are yet speaking, I will hear" (Isaiah 65:24).

August 1, 1965, was the date set for leaving Fort Campbell. I took seven days' leave the week before to find a place for Patty and the children. We settled on Wheaton, Illinois, since both of us had graduated from college there and still had friends in the little community twenty-five miles west of Chicago.

Back at Fort Campbell we engaged movers to pack and ship our goods, assured that they would be in Wheaton before Patty arrived. Then we rented a little three-room house designed for officers at Fort Campbell in transit between assignments.

On the eve of my departure the children sensed that this was our last day together. We spent a quiet evening enjoying each other. Matt and I walked over to a Little League ball game and had some cokes and popcorn. We went home and played games together, and then it was time for bed. That night we spent a little longer than usual "talking to Jesus." Matt asked Him to take care of Daddy; Sarah mumbled something only she and God understood; and then they both went to sleep.

At three the next morning everyone rolled out. Patty planned to get an early start in order to meet the movers in Wheaton by midday. At three-thirty she was ready to leave.

Those few moments are stamped forever on my memory. I can still feel the emptiness that swept over me, the creeping aloneness that only the companionship of one's family can dispel, the helplessness and uncertainty that persisted as I considered an unknown and hostile future. Not given to tears, I found they came quite easily as I hugged and kissed my children and remembered that it would be a year before I held them again. A year—if ever. As for Patty, she kept her tears for the long, anxious months ahead.

The predawn sky was filled with fog. There was a chill in the air. I stood in the dismal darkness and watched the car drive away. My family was gone.

A few hours later I climbed aboard the transport carrier for an eight-hour flight to San Francisco, regrouping emotionally on the way. It had been a good first year for me as a chaplain. The frictions and frustrations had been good for me. Now, facing the unknown, I once again offered to the Lord my ministry, my family and the coming year.

Almost immediately He began to move.

2

Farewell, My Country

It is the soldier's lot to make his home where he can find it, and ours at the end of our flight from Fort Campbell was the USS "Thomas A. Mann," a World War II troop carrier anchored in Oakland, California. The old bounder lay at rest, but its new boarders tossed and rolled that first night, sleeping the half-sleep of strangers in new quarters far from home.

Most of two whole engineer battalions poured steadily into the pipe-and-canvas "dorms" right up to our departure. A three-day delay quickly turned excitement into impatience.

"Let's get this show on the road!"

"What are we waiting for—Christmas?"

On land, the bay cities were reeling under the impact of the emotional "Vietniks" of Berkeley. Collegians and other youth with conspicuous garb and uncontrolled passions had launched an offensive assault on all troops arriving in Oakland en route to Southeast Asia. Trains were stopped as bearded protesters in sockless sneakers and smelly sweatshirts stretched themselves defiantly across the tracks. Pale, unkempt girls screamed obscene and blasphemous oaths at "LBJ's hired killers." One demonstrator straddled the handrail of a pullman, demanding from a young sergeant his reason for going to Vietnam.

"Lady," the GI calmly replied, "I'm going to Vietnam to preserve your right to make an ass of yourself."

The protests seemed to backfire. The noisier the demonstrations, the more our men were determined to go to battle—to fight—and to win.

The whole scene stripped away any illusions of grandeur I may have had about going off to war. There were no bands, no cheers—just loud voices of disenchantment on ship and on shore. We were permitted to disembark for brief periods within the vicinity of the "Mann." I must have called home half a dozen times—each call to be the "last" good-bye.

In the afternoon of August 5, 1965, a long, low whistle from the USS "Thomas A. Mann" signaled our departure for the bounding main. The engines answered with a roar and a shudder and soon the flotsam and jetsam of harbor scum were slipping past our hull. And then we were a mere speck on a vast ocean with a precious cargo of human lives to be hurled against a relentless enemy. Many on board would never see the homeland again.

My roommate was Raphael Benjamin, our battalion surgeon. I think we helped make the trip tolerable for each other, his Judaism and my Christianity adding dimensions of stimulating religious interest during the monotonous voyage. We were poles apart in convictions but close as personal friends. Dr. Ben objected to my one-way-of-salvation-through-Christ-Jesus approach; I argued against his sincere-goodworks formula for personal salvation, pressing upon him the

Communists, all the communities of the South Pacific would be endangered. But if they can be governed by democratic regimes, these countries can act as a restraining force, containing especially the political hunger of Red China.

When democracy is challenged by Communism anywhere, the United States of America is challenged. So are all people who give allegiance to justice and freedom. The Vietnam conflict may seem to be a far-off, remote involvement. It is not. It is rather an attempt to cut the spreading tentacles of a Communist menace before they reach to our shores and engulf us.

Most men understood the issues and were willing to participate in the war largely because of their appreciation of what they were leaving behind. Those who had difficulty needed only a few days in Vietnam to understand why we were there.

Halfway on our journey across the Pacific we learned that Qui Nhon was to be the new home of the 70th Engineer Battalion. Gone immediately were all humdrum and boredom. The troops, issued new Army Post Office numbers, began writing families and friends so they could expect mail on the distant shore.

Disembarkation was scheduled for five o'clock Monday morning, August 23. We held regular Sunday services and wound up our last Bible study. Then came the long night as we waited for a glimpse of the battlefield. No one slept much. The ship had gained time on the voyage and was now at a crawl. The sea, true to its name, was placid and calm. The air was humid and stuffy. There was no breeze. There was nothing to do but wait.

I went up to the top deck and peered into the blackness. From time to time I could dimly see bursts of red and yellow on the horizon. As we drifted closer I could hear the dull thud of artillery as the shells found their mark. I borrowed a tape recorder from a friend and sat down to share with Patty my feelings of controlled fear mingled with the fascination and wonder of it all.

There is deep curiosity, especially among the uninitiated, about war. Death is one absolute and demonstrable reality that every man must face. And every man wonders about it en route to war. The soldier is concerned about how he will die and whether he will "die well." In war, no professional military man wants to be on the second team; he wants to be where the action is and that is where the dying is. Perhaps it is through this door that existentialism made entry to the minds of Americans—even those of Christian believers.

The long, hot night gradually yielded to the first fingers of dawn that inched upward toward the sky. And then suddenly there lay Qui Nhon, muddy, thatched-roofed and sleepy.

These strange little brown people we had come so far to help, who were they?

3

History in Brown Faces

As it has for centuries, Vietnam moves on the backs of its people. They are sturdy backs propelled by swift feet and loaded by frugal hands.

The sands of their history have flowed through a turbulent glass. Their political feelings run deep. An oft-quoted adage of a Vietnamese nationalist goes something like this: "If the lord oppressed the people, he no longer deserved to be accepted as the lord. His person was no longer sacred, and to kill him was no longer a crime. Revolt against such tyranny was not only reasonable, it was a meritorious act which conferred upon the revolutionary the right to seize the power to rule."

With the possible exception in recent times of the so-called "miracle years" under Diem and the Thieu-Ky administration, the government of Vietnam has been in a constant state of turbulence, indecision and flux. Revolution has been the *modus operandi,* yet to view these people and live among them is to believe just the opposite.

Vietnamese have the typical Oriental show of kind

obeisance, yet with our hosts it was deeper. Their
genuine warmth is a quality kindled by the fire of suffering and adversity. Tribulation has indeed worked
patience. They seem never to hurry, always finishing
their work. Their extreme poverty has produced an
admirable frugality. About eight cents a day supplies
enough rice for a family of four, although many families are barely able to earn even that pittance.

One of the most remarkable qualities of the Vietnamese is their incredible endurance. They are small
but extremely hardy. Stories are still circulated about
the Viet Minh's struggle against the French. These in-
trepid people were able to dismantle a number of
captured French artillery pieces and lug them, along
with the hefty artillery shells, over miles of mountains
and jungles to positions where they were used against
the French at Dien Bien Phu in 1954. Even today, logistics experts determine that when any 81mm mortar
round is fired by the Viet Cong in South Vietnam it
means that for three months some indomitable soul
carried it on his back over the infamous Ho Chi Minh
trail to the battle. In the face of such formidable lo-
gistical obstacles, one wonders how the war has managed to last as long as it has! Fortunately, this quality
is shared by our South Vietnamese allies.

It is the policy of the United States Army to hire as
many loyal nationalists as possible. They serve as KPs
and waitresses in mess halls and clubs. The more
skilled are employed too and given assignments accordingly. In Bien Hoa a Vietnamese mason helped to
build a cement wall around our chapel. Pound for
pound, he was difficult to beat in aptitude for sheer
hard work.

A familiar sight along the country road or city
street is the hardy little Vietnamese, half bouncing,
half galloping along under a *don ganh* (carrying

pole) with a rice basket on each end filled to the brim
with anything from rice to squealing pigs or clucking
chickens. The pole with baskets is a symbol which
Vietnamese often use to describe their country. It rep-
resents the fertile rice-producing deltas of the Red
River in the North and the Mekong Delta in the
South, connected by a narrow strip of mountain and
plateau country.

There are 127,300 square miles. The 1962 popula-
tion was estimated to be approximately 30.5 million—
North Vietnam claiming 16.5 million and South Vietnam, 14 million.

The entire Indo-Chinese peninsula was probably in-
habited originally by an Austro-Indonesian people
much like those found in New Guinea today, according to most anthropologists. The physical distinctions
are noticeable, especially when compared with the
Chinese of whom more than a million have been given
citizenship in South Vietnam. The Chinese hold stra-
tegic financial positions in the country, such as bank-
ers and merchants, playing an important role in history as well as in current affairs of Vietnam.

Legend tells the story of a Prince Lac-Long Quan
who married a fairy named Au-Co about 2000 B.C.
Au-Co laid a hundred eggs, each of which hatched a
son. The sons split into two groups of fifty each. One
group went with their mother to the mountains of the
North, the other accompanied their father south to
the Red River delta country of South Vietnam. Then
began a series of Chinese conquests that lasted more
than a thousand years.

Maps issued by Red China today show much of
Southeast Asia—including Vietnam, Cambodia, Laos,
Thailand, Burma and many other countries—is consi-
dered a part of China. Mao Tse-tung intends to estab-

lish once again the "historic" China, including all the countries once ruled by this giant.

The Vietnamese first rebelled against China in A.D. 40 when sister queens Trung-Trac and Trung-Nhi led troops against Chinese garrisons and overthrew them. In angry retaliation the Chinese fought back, overrunning the queens' armies who in turn committed suicide rather than face their conquerors. The Trung sisters are worshiped as gods even today, despite their defeat.

Dynasties rose and fell until A.D. 959 when Ngo-Quyen drove out the Chinese and established home rule. He set up political machinery for a series of ruling dynasties which spanned a millennium. During this period the Vietnamese made a highly successful venture in colonialism which in 1672 led to Vietnamese control of all of South Vietnam, including Saigon. The city was formerly part of the Indianized Champa Kingdom founded in A.D. 192. The expansion of Vietnam continued to creep westward, gobbling up Cambodia too. In 1845 rebellion of the colonies brought about a condominium which remained until the French protectorate was established in 1863.

Actually, French rule began with the 1772 uprisings led by three brothers from Tay-son, a small village near An Khe on the northeastern edge of the Southern Mountain Plateau. Nguyen Anh, the last surviving prince of the Nguyen family, fought bitterly against the Tay-son rebellion and eventually emerged the victor with the help of a French "military advisory group." Prince Nguyen Anh then proclaimed himself emperor in 1802, adopting the name of Gia-Long. He gave the country its present name of Vietnam ("Southern Country of the Viet").[1] Gia-Long's regime

---

[1]*Viet* is the traditional word used for the people of Vietnam. *Nam* denotes their location—south of their Chinese descendants.

spanned Vietnam's long reach from the ancient to the present, since he was the direct ancestor of Emperor Bao-Dai whose regime was replaced by Ngo Dinh Diem in 1954.

The French, it is generally conceded, were in near absolute control of Indochina by 1884. Local government was visible, but it was only a political front. France held the reins in the hands of the French resident general. Its motives for colonialism were shared by other western Europeans, all in an attempt to open the Orient to Western trade.

French residency continued with little resistance until modern times. In 1905 the Vietnamese did receive a psychological shot in the arm by the defeat of Russia at the hands of the Japanese, shattering the myth of the invincibility of European powers. Some minor attempts by the Vietnamese to duplicate the victory of their "Japanese brother" flared up against the French but they were easily suppressed.

French prestige, lost in the 1905 Russian defeat, was regained by the Allied victory in World War I. The conflict introduced an unprecedented prosperity to Vietnam. Trade increased, the standard of living rose, schools opened, intellectuals were developed, as ideas, rather than people and things, became points of conversation. But the fruit of the vineyard was not all sweet.

By 1925 the political and intellectual climate had produced the Revolutionary Party of Young Annam, composed both of nationalists and Communists. This party became the forerunner of the League for Vietnam Independence, or the "Viet Minh." It emerged in 1939 under the leadership of Nguyen-Ai-Quoc, known today as Ho Chi Minh.

The French government collapsed during World War II at home and in its colonies, leaving a vacuum in Vietnam which was filled by the Japanese until their own defeat in 1945. At that time Ho Chi Minh declared Vietnam an independent republic.

Ironically, the United States furnished large shipments of arms and ammunition to the Viet Minh during World War II in the struggle against the Japanese. Consequently, many of the captured weapons taken from the Viet Cong in the recent conflict bear the stamp "Made in USA." M-1 rifles, carbines, Browning automatic rifles, 30- and 50-caliber machine guns and 57mm recoilless rifles made in our factories were being used to kill our boys. Since mid-1965, however, the enemy has been completely equipped by the Communists with a family of new and modern weapons.

By 1946 the French were in a position to reoccupy Vietnam, and they did, but not without the resistance of the Viet Minh—tough cadres directed by Ho Chi Minh through the military masterminding of General Vo Nguyen Giap.

The latter planned the strategy of the Viet Cong against the United States and South Vietnamese forces, but his recent offensives against the United States have not been as successful as they were against the French.

After their reoccupation in Indochina, French policy was to hold the area with a relatively small ground force. Under no circumstances were they to take heavy casualties. This forced them into a defensive campaign against a highly mobile, dedicated guerrilla force that gnawed and chewed, hit and ran, battered and beleaguered until on May 8, 1954, the French went down in total and inglorious defeat at Dien Bien Phu.

The war ended on July 21, 1954. Published casualty reports by the French showed losses in excess of

172,000 men. Once again a political vacuum prevailed and Ho Chi Minh seemed to be the only one on the horizon to fill it.

The Geneva Conference had been in session since April 26, 1954, called together to bring about a cease-fire in Vietnam. With a victory at Dien Bien Phu, the Communists brought to the negotiations a loud, determined voice, but an armistice was reached and Vietnam divided much like Korea the year before. All the territory north of the 17th parallel went to the Viet Minh. And all the territory south was to be under the presidency of Ngo Dinh Diem, who refused to sign the convention's agreement to partition the country. The United States also refused to sign this agreement.

Diem himself had done some politicking in the United States prior to assuming his nation's premiership in 1954, and had attracted the attention and backing of such men as Cardinal Spellman, Supreme Court Justice William O. Douglas, Senators Mike Mansfield and John F. Kennedy. Being an arch anti-Communist, Diem seemed to be the best political bet for the United States to champion in its endeavor to halt Communist expansion and aggression.

United States political and economic interest in Indochina preceded World War II, but we are there today primarily as a check against a terroristic overrun of Southeast Asia by Communism.

The question is often asked, Why should we bear the bulk of the burden of a people so remote? Why should the blood of young American manhood be shed for a people and land so far away?

Cain voiced a similar sentiment when he demanded, "Am I my brother's keeper?" to which the remainder of the Bible replies, "You are!"

Too few are the nations that will include in their practicing foreign policy the sentiments of the Saviour, "Love thy neighbour as thyself." Of course the inevitable question is the one asked by the lawyer in the gospel according to St. Luke, chapter 10: "And who is my neighbour?" Our Lord replied by giving the parable of the good Samaritan, teaching that anyone in need is our neighbor. Therefore He said, "Go thou and do likewise."

Being a neighbor obviously goes beyond the limits of those who live in the house next door. It exceeds the bounds of geographical proximity.

Are we not our Vietnam brothers' keepers?

4

"Happy Valley"

I half expected to leap off the landing craft in Qui Nhon and heroically dive for cover behind a tree or mound of sand to escape the blazing guns of the Viet Cong, but such was not the case.

Instead, as little children scampered about shouting and laughing, our commanding officer led us off the landing craft in military formation, our flags and battle streamers flowing meekly in the still, warm air. Not a shot was fired, not a Viet Cong seen.

Our new home lay halfway between the 17th parallel, which divides North and South Vietnam, and Saigon. Qui Nhon rested in comparative ruins compared with the days when discriminating tourists called it the "Riviera of the Orient." Now the tourists had given place to refugees from North Vietnam and the beautiful seaside hotels to overpopulated mud-and-bamboo huts with wash dangling from drooping clotheslines.

Drab olive military vehicles were everywhere, but the populace ignored them in the daily conduct of business. Women in cone-shaped hats and beautiful *au-dis* (sheath dresses) moved about gracefully along streets that were strewn with maggot-ridden fish heads, human refuse and rusted pieces of burned-out French armored cars.

Children were everywhere—in the streets, on the beach, in the water. Open sewers drained into the bay, reeking with nauseating smells that hung like fog over the entire city. Smoke from charcoal cooking fires fed by pungent Oriental herbs joined the riot of odors. Older women with black teeth and bad breath caused by chewing the betelnut scurried about. Half-naked children with bloated bellies squatted to relieve themselves whenever and wherever the urge was felt. But after the initial shock of it all, adjustment came rapidly.

Prior to our off-loading from the USS "Mann," Major Richard Robinson, our Battalion S-3 in charge of training and operations, met us on our Landing Craft Utility and briefed us on procedures such as our route of march to our assigned bivouac area following our off-loading from the landing craft. There was little about the entire scene to suggest that a war was going on except the occasional hum of an old World War II propeller-driven A-IE Skyraider which the US Air Force had furnished to South Vietnamese pilots.

Despite the calm, or perhaps because of it, there was a feeling of excited cautiousness. By the time the battalion was finally assembled on the shore our chief concern seemed to be getting something to eat. My assistant and I got in line for our C rations. Our table was the hood of a jeep, and we bowed to give thanks for our first meal in combat zone. After the meal we planned and executed our move to bivouac in suburban Qui Nhon.

My assistant had no trouble finding our jeep and we took our place in the motor march which was to take us through the heart of the city. We had a queasy feeling and I instructed my assistant to keep moving—to stop only if it became absolutely necessary. We were, I am certain, much more nervous and concerned than were the Vietnamese. The GI was becoming a familiar sight to the inhabitants of Qui Nhon.

Major Richard Robinson had reconnoitered and chosen for our area a sandy stretch of twenty acres wrapped like a half-moon around a rocky finger outcropping from the mountains of the Central Highlands. American Marines occupied the high ground above us, offering a measure of security in the area.

We arrived at our rock-strewn, scrubby home early in the afternoon and studied small strip maps showing tentative location assignments of the companies and the sections of battalion headquarters. The chapel area was conspicuously located leeward of a small sandy bluff, exactly where it should have been—next to the troops and on the main access road to the battalion area.

I spent that apprehensive first night in a pup tent shared by Dr. Benjamin, our battalion surgeon. Fortunately, the most serious incident was the attack of a persistent mosquito inspired, no doubt, by the Viet Cong.

Everyone remained on edge for the first several nights in Qui Nhon. One of the men on guard duty detected movement to the side of his station and called out, "Halt!" Receiving no reply, he fired twice with precision marksmanship and learned afterward he had shot a buddy coming to relieve him at the guard post. The victim said he didn't hear the call before the shots. One round broke his shoulder and the other his arm, but the soldier was flown to Hawaii immediately and later recovered fully.

Episodes like this are by far the exception rather

than the rule, but they always attract much attention when they occur. They are one of the occupational hazards of warfare. Occasionally our own forces are hit by friendly air and artillery strikes, but the incidents are so infrequent they don't even lend themselves to a percentage study. Seldom are the accidents the result of human error. No human intervention, for example, can prohibit an inherently faulty artillery round from falling short of its mark.

For the Christian, these "accidents" have a different meaning. A sovereign God in absolute control directs not only the enemy's "arrows that fly by day" (Psalm 91:5) but also the "arrows" of his own company. The year in Vietnam convinced me that there is no such thing as a bullet inscribed "To whom it may concern." God alone determines the length of a man's days.

On our second day in the combat zone we were up before dawn. My mission was to provide a chapel for my men but materials assigned were late in coming. I had expected to conduct services from the hood of a jeep, but our farsighted and industrious S-4 (officer in charge of supplies and logistics), Mr. Hansen, had provided for us a large wall tent seventy by twenty-three feet for the purpose. But it would be some time before we would actually get it.

To build and equip my tabernacle in the wilderness I had to use a little creative initiative. Lumber we found in abundance from pine boards of all sizes used to pack our equipment. We needed an altar, a pulpit and something for the men to sit on.

I felt I was in danger of wearing out my welcome but the need for a chapel convinced most benefactors that my cause was just, my mission necessary. My assistant and I built the altar and the pulpit. "Charlie" Company volunteered to build the "pews."

Over our four-cornered lean-to my assistant and I

stretched two rain-repellent ponchos at the close of our first day. We built a wooden cross with hammer and nails and painted it white. Then we hauled our gear inside and there I prepared to spend the night.

Drowsily approaching sleep, I was suddenly jolted awake by muffled sobs coming from my assistant's tent a few feet away. I sat up and strained to hear. There was no mistake, the soldier was crying. Not loudly or uncontrollably, but definitely crying.

"Irv," I called, "are you all right?"

The sobbing continued. I got out of bed and crept cautiously toward the tent. In the blackness of the night I knelt down and pulled back the tent flaps.

"Irv! Are you all right?"

This time the sobbing came to a choking halt. "I'm sorry, sir, I just can't help it."

Crawling inside, I knelt by his bed. Irvin Herner had been my assistant for nearly a year, and he had been a good one. Besides handling the administrative duties of the chapel with dispatch, he kept the chapel in good order and assisted me in many ways. A committed Christian, Irv brought to his work an added dimension of evangelistic zeal coupled with compassion and concern for the individual. He had been brought to Christ through the life and ministry of a layman in a small Christian and Missionary Alliance church in Pennsylvania. Recently married, and only twenty-three years old, Irv had been earnestly seeking God's place for his life of service. That night he found it.

"What's the trouble, Irv?"

"It's these people, sir," he said. "They have absolutely nothing and besides, they are living in darkness. They need Christ but there are so few to tell them."

He sat up in his bunk. "I've been watching them,"

he said, "and I'm overwhelmed at their need. I could never live in the United States again with all that prosperity, knowing the physical and financial and—above all—the spiritual poverty of these people."

Now the tears stopped. His voice came clear and determined as he spoke of the people he had so recently met. "Lord willing, I'll come back here when I get out of the Army," Irv said. "And once I do, I don't think I'll ever be able to leave."

I suggested we pray together and that he offer his decision to the Lord for His guidance. When we rose from our knees, Irv confided: "You know, sir, ever since I became a Christian I've been waiting for the Lord to show me what He has for me. Tonight, for the first time, I can say I have a real purpose in life and I can hardly wait to get on with it!"

That was August 25, 1965. By the time I left the battalion in early November Irv had acquired a Vietnamese language guide and gained a halting conversational facility with the people. Able to make himself understood, he had started his own civic-action program by assisting in many refugee centers of the area. He invested his spare time in service with the local Christian and Missionary Alliance missionaries, observing and helping where he could. There were times when I had to curtail his enthusiasm to make sure our chapel program functioned properly.

The last I heard of Irvin Herner he was planning to enroll in Nyack Missionary College, Nyack, New York, with the goal of returning to Vietnam with his wife as soon as possible.

By the end of a week our chapel was ready for services. A wooden pulpit above an altar with sheets of woven straw around it, a partition to separate the sanctuary from my living quarters, and then a white bed sheet from the battalion aid station to drape over the altar on which I placed the appointments from my chaplain's kit to create a worshipful setting.

Irv had learned to play our little field organ and this contributed greatly to the services. The intense humidity made the keys swell and stick, so Irv had to pull some first echelon maintenance on it before each meeting.

In my living quarters we built a desk and wash-stand and touched them up with white paint.

Despite the absence of pews, we had more men out that Sunday than had ever come to services in Fort Campbell. God used the combat situation to bring men to Himself. I addressed them with a message ti-tled "Worship Before Warfare," based on chapter 6 of Joshua where the biblical general deals with Israel's stunning victory over Jericho and the unconventional techniques used in the overthrow. Most important to the lesson are the last few verses of chapter 5 describ-ing Joshua's confrontation with the captain of the ar-mies of the Lord whom many believe to be the prein-carnate Son of God. Joshua's response to this en-counter was to fall on his face in worship.

The lesson was clear and well received as I told my men, "We must prepare ourselves spiritually through an encounter with Jesus Christ before we are fully prepared for the battlefield."

I tried to make all my messages relevant to a mili-tary situation and was amazed to discover how much of the Scriptures is concerned with battles, conflicts and wars—especially the Old Testament. More im-portant, I discovered the unfailing preservation and protection that God promises to His own. The entire history of Israel and the psalms of David abound with such teaching. Suitable texts were not hard to find.

Now it was time to unpack a large Conex container

filled with Christian literature brought from home. We built a table and stocked it with material furnished by the Billy Graham Crusade headquarters. Sincere Christians helped finance a shipment of tracts written by J. B. Phillips. By the time all this was ready for shipment from Fort Campbell it weighed well over a thousand pounds.

As soon as it was on display, word got out and the rush was on. In this manner we drew many new men from surrounding units into the chapel services. We had only one requirement, spelled out in bold type in a sign above the table: "Take all you want, but read all you take. Then pass it on." There was enough for all, and no one was denied the item he requested. As always, the Lord provided just what we needed.

My situation was ideal for any chaplain: a chapel with regular services, an office, designated living area, a reservoir of literature. All this in a combat zone seemed too good to be true. It couldn't last—and it didn't!

Ten days after our arrival Lieutenant Colonel Leonard Edelstein, our commanding officer, called an unscheduled staff meeting to advise that two of our companies would leave by truck convoy in two days for An Khe, a small village to the west on Route 19. Our mission was to give engineer assistance to an advance party of the 1st Air Cavalry Division which was to establish its home base in An Khe. This was a crash project, since the 1st Cavalry was due in September and it was already nearly the end of August. Roads had to be cut, culverts built, bridges constructed and a multitude of other details cared for before a unit of that size could move in.

On Wednesday, September 2, 1965, the lead elements of the two designated companies moved out from "Happy Valley," the name we fondly attached to our base camp at Qui Nhon. Battalion Headquarters, Headquarters Company and one line company remained at Qui Nhon.

The following Sunday I too moved out. A helicopter took me to An Khe to hold services for our men there. They were in good spirits, working by shifts around the clock, driven by the pressure of deadlines. They recognized the urgency and accepted its challenge.

Our services were held in the mess tents of each company, drawing all available personnel—even company commanders.

Present at An Khe was Lieutenant Ted Yates, a real hard charger who commanded Alpha Company of the 70th. He attended the service and helped to promote the chapel program. Afterward he invited me over to his tent for lunch. Ted was a dedicated man, not only to the Army but also to the Saviour. This twin devotion was apparent to all who talked to him. Lieutenant Yates was concerned not only with doing a good job as a professional soldier but in molding the character of his men as well. He believed one could not be done without the other. This man's man confirmed my own persuasion that a commander, or any soldier, doesn't have to be some kind of religious odd-wad to stand up for his convictions and encourage his men to do the same.

After the day's services and some milling around with the men I caught a flight back to Qui Nhon. Our pilot swooped low over the awesome Deo Mang Pass so we could see the sobering ambush sites that lay conveniently at every turn. I felt that it would be just a matter of time before I would have to travel that dangerous route through the pass. It came sooner than I had expected.

On Tuesday next another staff meeting was called

by the commanding officer. The inevitable was about to occur. The entire unit was moving to An Khe to be in direct support of the 1st Air Cavalry Division. It seemed logical, since the 1st Cavalry had no combat engineers organic to them with our equipment and capability. Also, there was no other unit in the area readily available to fill the bill. The mission was ours more by the process of elimination than by anything else.

Our officers seemed excited about the order, since it would involve us with a unit considered by many to be the hottest thing in modern warfare. Much was at stake for the 1st Cavalry. Theirs was a new concept of warfare—helicopter warfare—and many people in high places were watching closely their operations. The concept had received a lot of publicity, and big decisions rode on their success or failure. Time, mobility and remarkable leadership have attested the concept's overwhelming success. Officers of the 70th Engineer Battalion, especially the commanding officer, could read the handwriting on the wall and were enthusiastic at the opportunity to be placed in direct support of the 1st Air Cavalry Division.

On Thursday, September 9, 1965, at 3:00 A.M., the remaining remnants of our battalion joined a truck convoy for the overland route to An Khe. Ahead lay forty-five miles of Viet Cong-infested territory climaxed by three and a half miles of dangerous, grueling uphill terrain through the Deo Mang Pass to the new home of the 70th Engineer Battalion.

Apprehensively, fortified by prayer such as we had never offered to God before, we began moving into the enemy's stronghold.

5

In the Spirit of
Mike Coursey

The formidable Deo Mang Pass yielded to the massive convoy containing units of the 70th Engineer Battalion now moving at a determined gait. The occasional crack of a sniper's high-powered rifle kept us constantly on the alert, but to everyone's amazement the move from Qui Nhon to An Khe was made without mishap. No ambushes, no pitched battles—just a few sniper rounds to let us know this was "Charlie's" home territory.

For many years the French army, as well as that of the South Vietnamese, had been unable to negotiate the pass; but Route 19, for all practical purposes, has not been closed since our escorted convoy went through in September, 1965. Scattered violations of exploding mines and occasional attempts to blow up a bridge have only briefly threatened the South Vietnamese and their allies, for the Viet Cong no longer control this scenic territory.

Now began the challenge of the battalion's stagger-

ing commitment. First, a twelve-mile, two-lane road
had to be built to provide access for units of the 1st
Air Cavalry Division into An Khe: Parking space for
their four hundred and fifty aircraft was just one requirement among many. No attempt was made to
confine ourselves to inadequate space because this
was Viet Cong territory.

Our battalion was accustomed to building roads,
bridges, culverts and airfields. The difficulty at An
Khe was the crushing deadline which allowed only
about fifteen days to complete the task. Officers and
enlisted men alike worked around the clock to meet
the deadline, accomplishing what Major General Kinnard, the commander of the 1st Air Cavalry Division,
called a "fantastic achievement." It was indeed that.

Our first Sunday came and still there was no permanent location for services. An army chaplain learns
early that he must "stay loose" and remember that
whatever the situation of the moment it will change—
sometimes rather abruptly. That Sunday we practiced
the art of flexibility. With the roar of bulldozers and
five-ton dump trucks just over the hill we had three
well-attended worship services in a beautiful little
meadow about half the size of a football field, encircled with palm trees and brilliant red flowers.

One week later we were back on schedule, established in our second chapel. The pulpit and altar were
in place; the organ had been dehumidified and was in
excellent playing condition; there were pews for the
men, built by volunteer labor from "Charlie"
Company.

For the occasion I told the story of Mike Coursey's
conversion.

Sp-4 Mike Coursey had been a medic with the 70th
Engineers at Fort Campbell. He was endowed with
an abundance of personal magnetism and charm. He

played a guitar better than the average instrumental-
ist and kept everyone in his barracks "swinging."
Mike was friendly and generous, always ready with a
smile and a dollar for a buddy whose budget had collapsed before payday. He was built like a halfback, if
perhaps a little light, but he made up in spirit what
he lacked in brawn.

I first met Mike during the fall football season of
1964 soon after joining the 70th Engineer Battalion at
Fort Campbell. Each company was forming a touch
football team for some friendly competition. Since I
had played football in high school and college, I decided to join the games and get acquainted with some
of the men.

Being the battalion chaplain, I was assigned to
headquarters company, and so was Mike Coursey. At
practice each afternoon I became well acquainted
with him and the other teammates. Mike attended the
Sunday chapel services infrequently, but he was always willing to help out any way he could.

Ten days before we were scheduled to leave Fort
Campbell, Mike went swimming with some friends in
a nearby town. He dived into shallow water and
broke his neck, suffering an injury that left him para-
lyzed permanently from his neck down.

My reaction was a stunning shock. *What a tragedy!*
A young man in life's bloom with such potential!
What a shame! But after talking with Mike as he lay
motionless in a hospital bed I changed my mind.

The young soldier was from Oklahoma. Before
coming into the Army he had been active in his
church but in the barracks he lost interest in spiritual
matters and began drifting from God.

When the doctor broke the news that he would
never recover from the accident he was bitter and de-
spondent, but not for long. Soon his heart began to

sing. He was actually thankful, he said, for what had happened because his relationship with God was dramatically reestablished.

"You know, Chaplain," he told me, "I wouldn't trade spots with any man in the world!"

With tears in his eyes he continued: "The Lord has made Himself more real to me through this accident than I ever believed possible.

"A lot of these guys in here are propositioning God. They're telling Him that if He'll heal them they will straighten up and live for Him. But you know what? Whether the Lord raises me up or not, I'm going to tell others about Him and His love if I have to pay someone to push me around in a bed for the rest of my life. Being healed is beside the point. I just want other people to know Him the way He has revealed Himself to me."

I listened, fascinated, as Mike continued: "There are times here at night when it's quiet and I'm wide awake that I feel like bursting with praise and joy. The presence of Jesus Christ is so real I can hardly contain myself. Don't pity me, Chaplain. And tell the boys not to feel sorry for me. I wouldn't trade what God has given me for anything."

The men in adjacent beds listening to Mike that day were deeply moved. So were the men now listening to the story in a Vietnam combat zone who, like Mike, were facing death and injury in battle. Three days after arriving in Vietnam we learned that Mike had died.

On September 19, 1965, we held our first service in our little house of worship. I recounted to a full house the story of Mike Coursey, relating the spectacular experiences of the Apostle Paul in Acts 9 to that of the soldier from Oklahoma. I stressed the point that God uses different means to bring men to Himself and

confronted the men with this question: "What would
God have to do to bring you to Himself?" My message made clear the ageless story of redemption
through faith in the Saviour, how Jesus Christ the Son
of God had paved the way by His death and resurrection so that each one of us can come boldly to Him
and accept pardon for sin.

The roster of weekly activities in the new Chapel
was jammed. Since it was the only chapel in the 1st
Cavalry area at the time of our arrival, it served the
Roman Catholics for Sunday mass, accommodated the
Jewish service every Friday evening and the Seventh-
day Adventists on Saturday. Mormons gathered at the
Chapel on Sunday afternoons at three o'clock.

Communion each Sunday, a particularly blessed
service for me, was added to chapel activities by request of the men. Once again improvising provided
cooled grape juice and a half loaf of bread from our
mess sergeant each Sunday. We passed a common
brass chalice from my chaplain's kit and each man
dipped his morsel of bread into the fruit of the grape
as we remembered again the Lord's death for us.

Here in combat my men had serious questions
about war and asked for biblical solutions. The strain
of living under tension brought many men to Tuesday
and Thursday evening Bible classes where we
searched the Scriptures like the Bereans of old.

"Doesn't the Bible say you shouldn't kill?" one GI
wanted to know. "How can we fulfill our responsibility as soldiers and still obey that commandment?"

As a chaplain, I was interested in this oft-repeated
question for two reasons. First, I was a member of the
Brethren Church which is traditionally nonresistant
though not pacifist. I wished to explain the difference:
The pacifist believes war is inherently wrong and will
take no part in it. The nonresistant fellow recognizes

the evil influences in world affairs and thus the inevitability of war, but usually he will serve in the armed forces—often as a noncombatant medic, truck driver or in the mess hall.

I showed the men many passages, especially in the Old Testament, where God gave specific instructions concerning battle:

Joshua was told by God to subdue Jerusalem, sparing not even the women and children (Joshua 6:1-5, 21).

Joshua's conquests of the city of Ai (8:1, 21), of Gibeon (10:10), and of Canaan (11:6, 9, 11-12, 15, 20) were all commanded by God.

God directed the battlefield victories of King Saul (I Samuel 11:6).

God's benediction was on Samuel as he "hewed Agag to pieces before the LORD in Gilgal" (I Samuel 15:33).

David's victories over Goliath and over the Syrians (II Samuel 10:18) were both under God's direction (I Samuel 17:31-51).

The commandment "Thou shalt not kill" was explained by comparing it with other passages of Scripture. In Matthew 5:21-22, Christ discusses the commandment, "Thou shalt not kill," in relation to an individual's motives and heart attitude. The Saviour marks the distinction between murder and the taking of life in general, as do all legal systems. Murder is defined in Article 118 in the Uniform Code of Military Justice, in the Manual for Courts-Martial, United States, 1951. Here it states that "the killing of a human being is unlawful when done without justification or excuse."

It further states that "the general rule is that the acts of a subordinate, done in good faith in compliance with his supposed duty or orders, are justifiable." The code hastens to add, however: "This justification does not exist when these acts are manifestly beyond the scope of his authority, or the order is such that a man of ordinary sense and understanding would know it to be illegal." This distinction between murder and killing is found in most legal systems throughout history.

Likewise, the Lord goes beyond the actual act of taking life to examine the motive behind the act. He teaches that if there is anger or malice aforethought in the heart, whether the act of actually taking a life is performed or not, the individual is in danger of judgment.[1] When a man hates, he has already committed murder in his heart. That is where the Lord looks to examine the motives and attitudes.

When projected to the battlefield, the principle remains the same. A soldier engaging the enemy with hate and malice thereby commits murder in his heart, placing himself "in danger of the judgment." My observations convince me that the soldier motivated by hate is not an efficient fighting man. His judgments are fogged; there is a recklessness about him that places not only himself but all those with him in jeopardy. The best fighting man is the one motivated by a sense of duty and responsibility in subjection to his government. The fact remains that God knows the heart and judges each man accordingly. The commandment "Thou shalt not kill" should not only prevent a Christian soldier from murder but should also motivate him to be willing to serve in the armed forces so as to help prevent others from such sin.

[1]See Genesis 9:6; Exodus 21:12.

As soldiers under the authority of our government, we gave attention to the Apostle Paul's instruction found in Romans 13. Here the sacred text teaches that God ordained and instituted governing authorities over the people of the world and that the governed were subject to this authority. The passage teaches also that God authorized the use of the sword by these powers for the protection and preservation of the good, as well as for the punishment of evildoers.

It is apparent that a Christian who subjects himself both to divine authority and to a God-ordained government may well find himself to be an extension of the arm of God that bears the sword.

For the one seeking the mind of God in bearing arms and taking life and in all other matters, the Bible abounds with guiding principles. The problem comes in relying solely on the wisdom and whims of man-made philosophies. There is no scriptural sympathy for the "revoltnik" whose mentality is seen in his motto "Make love, not war."

For the man of God, however, the still, small voice of the Spirit directs, "This is the way, walk ye in it."

6

The Answer's in the Man

The face of our enemy had changed. The arsenal we now faced was climatic. Mother Nature and her monsoons were his weapons. Against this most formidable foe marched a battalion of invincible American engineers armed with D-handled shovels—the only weapon yet designed to bring him to his knees. A continuous, persistent rain fed by the monsoons turned Vietnam into a giant quagmire. It was a notable achievement for a soldier to remain only moderately miserable in this jungle of water.

Day after day the glowering skies kept up their watery barrage until everything was wet. A chest of drawers made for me by a carpenter in An Khe quickly swelled shut. The trenches around our tents had to be redug every day to accommodate the small rivers. Tents and makeshift shelters which served as sleeping quarters quickly developed big leaks. A pool and then a gully formed in the chapel, carrying the brown water right down the middle of our sanctuary. Only an elaborate drainage system kept the whole tent from washing away. We struggled every day just to maintain what had been constructed. And yet culverts washed out, bridges gave way, roads simply disappeared, large army vehicles were swallowed up in mud.

During this moisturized nightmare I increased my efforts to stay close to the men. Part of the chaplain's job is to be informed about the morale of his men and to keep his commander informed about any extreme ups and downs. At least once a day, sometimes more often, I visited the job sites and projects to talk with the men in their monsoon misery.

On one of these trips around the perimeter road circling the area I came upon a washed-out culvert. Three of our men were working feverishly to redirect the water, at the same time trying to convince some GIs from another unit that they should not try to cross the flooded area. These GIs had just returned from a trip to An Khe and bore evidence that their pass had been spent in some of its bars. The engineers, waging "war" with their D-handled shovels, were having no more success with the men than with the water. Both were out of control.

Despite the shouts and warnings and commands, one of the inebriates proceeded gingerly into the stream. The current would have knocked down a strong man in complete control of his faculties, but for a "well oiled" GI it was only a matter of seconds before the inevitable happened. After four steps into the rushing stream the tipsy soldier was in over his head, being viciously whisked downstream by the water.

A quick survey revealed that I was the only one who could swim, so I went in—boots and all—to rescue the hapless GI. Once when I was working as a lifeguard back home I had helped bring in two men who had almost drowned. But trying to handle a man who was under the influence of liquor presented an altogether different set of problems. The GI weighed at least two hundred pounds. On top of that he was scared and sick. Rather than fight him and the current I struggled just to keep our heads above the water while maneuvering in the direction of the shore. About a hundred yards downstream from where he fell in we finally made it. The poor soldier had passed out from exhaustion and I am sure I would have done the same thing had the struggle gone on much longer.

Fortunately, as we had been carried downstream in the water the other men had run alongside and were there to help carry our victim back. He was sober now and shaking from the cold and fear, but actually he was no worse for the wear.

Then suddenly with a jolt we discovered that another man from his group had disappeared. We called the MPs and notified a nearby dispensary. Just as we were about to pull away to get an ambulance, our long-lost friend appeared—and how he did appear! He looked something like a ludicrous version of Venus rising from the sea. As he stepped out of the water he was wearing combat boots, a pistol belt and a steel helmet. No more, no less. His motives had been good. Above the roar of the water he yelled, "Whersh my buddy? Shomebody help me find my buddy!" His other friends were able to corral him before he too stepped back into the washout.

Frequently I am asked by spiritually sensitive persons about the off-duty practices and morality of our men under arms. Having served both with a peacetime army as well as with combat forces, I know some of the problems and believe that certain observations can be safely made.

A soldier's morality begins long before he becomes a soldier. If the formative environments of his home and church have made positive moral contributions in his early life, then they will invariably be reflected in his conduct in the armed services. The army itself never made a bum out of a man. In fact, the Army has been known not infrequently to make a man out of a bum.

"It is not the service that causes a man to yield," one officer put it. "It is the man who causes himself to yield." The service provides an environment in which latent attitudes and desires can become overt. The soldier can proceed in any moral direction he chooses. If he had some half-hidden hostility to the church and its message, the military will provide the opportunity for its release. If his faith was superficial and ungrounded, then it will probably be dropped after his first encounter with a determined libertine.

The key is not the Army. The key is the man—his upbringing and depth of commitment before entering the service. A young man committed to a life of exemplary moral behavior may find the Army challenging that commitment, but rarely will the Army change it. A young man with convictions that are not personal, but rather conditioned by family and community pressures on him to conform, will be less likely to stand when these pressures on him are removed.

A man can find anything he wants at a military installation in peacetime or in war. That's true of every man in every city in the world, whether he is a soldier or not. A man can find worthless trinkets, prostitutes or an endless variety of bars. Or he can find valuable gems, good friends and good times that he will not have to regret later. The civilian or the soldier has only to choose what he wants, and there is little a police officer or military commander can do about it unless he is caught breaking the law or military regulations.

A vivid case in point was the so-called "Disneyland" on the outskirts of An Khe. Unfortunately a good name was degraded by affixing it to a place for organized prostitution which received undue publicity in various news media. "Disneyland" sprang into existence while General Harry W. O. Kinnard was the commanding general of the 1st Air Cavalry Division, so he bore the brunt of undue criticism. The general is a "practicing" Christian, faithful in church attendance and in encouraging his men to do likewise. He always demonstrated an active concern for the whole chapel program. The presence of such a place as "Disneyland" in a foreign country has no connection with the leadership of one man—certainly not that of General Kinnard.

Six weeks after American troops arrived in An Khe the venereal disease rate rose alarmingly. Long ago the Army abolished punitive measures regarding VD. Punishment only drove it underground as men refused to seek treatment until they were in an advanced stage of disease. The solution has been to encourage the contaminated man to seek treatment immediately with no overt reprisal. I say "overt" reprisal, because word always seems to get back to the man's sergeant or commanding officer and the errant man may find himself with no passes and with more KP and guard duty than usual.

In An Khe, the specter of the treacherous disease once again loomed its ugly head. Bars had sprung up overnight when the troops arrived, each saloon featuring its own parade of prostitutes. Even barbershops and laundries provided this extra "service" for weak-willed GIs. Something had to be done quickly.

General Kinnard's first tactic was to place the entire village of An Khe "off limits" to all military personnel. Almost immediately loud cries of protest came from the legitimate merchants in the village who had purchased large supplies of merchandise to sell to the soldiers. Vietnam's local economic posture has been and continues to be one of the major factors which permit the Communists to gain a foothold in a village, then in a town, then in a district. To shut off the village to all Americans seemed to play right into Red hands.

Village authorities came to General Kinnard with the "Disneyland" plan. It was they who suggested an area be set aside exclusively for the practice of prostitution. Doctors would give weekly examinations and treatment would be made available immediately when disease was detected. Prostitution would be illegal in any other place. If rules were broken, An Khe would again be stamped "off limits" to the GIs.

Inevitably, the morality of such action was questioned. But this issue, like many others, did not ask whether prostitution was to be practiced. It *would* continue. The question was one of control—control of the disease. Control is not tantamount to approval. Many of these who had the deepest objections on moral and spiritual grounds were the first to see that control was necessary.

If the entire village of An Khe had been placed off limits, an entirely new set of moral questions and problems would have arisen. A comparable case in point is the prohibition era a generation or more ago in the United States. Spiritually sensitive, godly people have been facing these issues for centuries. The world at large will not allow itself to be controlled and restrained by scriptural guidelines. Solutions have to be presented which check and control those who need it most but want it least.

Prohibition was a noble effort by a moral constituency to banish a social ill, but it served only to usher in an unparalleled period of history plagued by every known brand of crime, lawlessness and depravity. The motives were pure, but the results disastrous. To legislate abstinence in the area of morals is difficult, if not impossible, business. However, controls and legal restraints in these areas are obviously necessary. Those who desire no controls seem to condone immorality, whereas those with a morally sensitive fiber are more likely to demand controls.

Criminologists and sociologists generally agree that one of the primary causes of crime and pathological social behavior is a demand for them. Gambling, prostitution, bootlegging and immorality thrive on a large scale because the public demands them. A businessman's understanding of the law of supply and demand largely determines success in a business. Legislation had served to hinder open, rampant immorality, but there will always be objections to Christian ethics by those who claim no allegiance to Christ. Personal regeneration still offers the only realistic hope for social reformation. This is outlined in Ephesians 4:22-25: "What you learned was to fling off the dirty clothes of the old way of living, which were rotted through and through with lust's illusions, and, with yourselves mentally and spiritually remade, to put on the clean fresh clothes of the new life which was made by God's design for righteousness and the holiness which is no illusion" (Phillips).

As a chaplain, it was my duty to serve all the men —good and bad, drunk and sober, promiscuous and faithful. It was my responsibility to seize opportunities and means to offer to each man the claims and provisions of Jesus Christ for an abundant life. Each was free to accept or to reject. I was free only to accept every man as he was and to hold out to him the promise of what he could be in Jesus Christ.

I met a number of Christian men in Vietnam who,

before coming into the Army, had nursed a streak of rebelliousness. Since their induction and first real contact with the extremes of sin they had been led to a depth of commitment to Christ that they had not known previously. The military environment offered them a challenge which they faced and mastered.

On a beautiful Sunday afternoon in October I had the privilege of baptizing a cluster of my men on the banks of the Be River north of An Khe. Some came only to watch with interest. One was my good friend, Dr. Benjamin. He was still convinced of his Jewish faith but was interested in the men and their Christian commitment. Others came simply as Christians to share the joys of other believers. And some came to be baptized. Some of the soldiers had been Christians for some time without taking this step, and now wished to make a public witness. But most of the candidates for baptism that day had trusted Christ since arriving in Vietnam with the military unit.

The first was my friend and assistant, Irvin Herner. For all of us there that afternoon, the mass declaration of faith in the risen Christ was indeed a moving experience, a mountaintop preceding the unknown valleys ahead.

While memory serves I shall never forget my men of the 70th Engineer Battalion. We had many hours of good times singing and playing and laughing together.

It was Barney Kelland, an architectural engineer who had come to the United States from Norway, who organized our first choir. It took both his hands and feet and concentration to play our foot-pumping military organ, however, so I was pressed into service to direct the group of male voices assembled.

Major Richard Robinson, our S-3, was a regular who took over the direction of the choir when I left.

Lieutenant Ted Yates was another unforgettable who always gave the rest of us a boost by his infectious enthusiasm.

A number of the men of the 70th began calling our nightly "hoots" the battalion's own "Grand Ole Opry." I'm sure we matched the Nashville group in noise, if not in musical skill.

My brief acquaintance with the guitar came in handy. We had brought no musical instruments with us, but our Vietnamese friends soon solved that problem when they learned that these strange American soldiers wanted to make music. They all but buried us in an avalanche of cheap, tinny Oriental stringed instruments. They were guitars, nonetheless, and we found that we could enjoy playing them *almost* as much as playing a hundred-dollar Gibson.

Sergeant Major Burnie Jetton, a man with a fine military career with airborne units with whom he had made more than six hundred jumps, provided "atmosphere" for our chapel by providing four snow-white reserve parachutes which we pinned to the top of our tent inside.

Throughout those many months with the 70th Engineers, God was always available to do His work in men's lives, including the chaplain's. Both the battalion and I were fortunate in having a commanding general of the 1st Air Cavalry Division who believed that the soldier's spiritual life was of great importance. Major General Kinnard arranged for a full-scale briefing by his staff of all chaplains under his command. When the staff had briefed us on the plans for the division, General Kinnard shared with us some cogent observations based upon his own experiences in three wars. He noted that the combat soldier, because of the nature of his task and the unpredictability of his immediate future, is more aware of the spiritual dimension of life than he might be otherwise. The general observed that men in combat tend to think about the shaping forces in their lives and to remember that the church contributed in some measure. He urged us to take every opportunity to be with the men and to gear our services to provide constructive, biblical solutions to the special problems and questions that the combat soldier always faces.

My year of service in Vietnam confirmed General Kinnard's remarks. Obviously, when a man is placed in a position where he must consider the possibility that his life may end in an instant, he goes further to ponder the ultimate questions: *What about life after death? Is there an eternity? Where will I spend it? Is is possible for man to have a personal relationship with God? Can I be sure about it for myself?*

The thought of a sniper's bullet or a mortar fragment turns many a man's mind almost instinctively to his Creator. Not, as General Kinnard pointed out, because of some foreboding dread or uncontrollable fear, but because of the soldier's realistic appraisal of the environment in which he must function.

Whatever the underlying causes of their thinking along these lines, my approach was to present Jesus Christ as the Saviour, the One who alone can deliver, protect and preserve a man's life.

When it comes to proclaiming Christ, the Army is no different from any other situation. Some who listen will reject the message. Some will say, as they did on Mars Hill to the Apostle Paul, "We will hear thee again on this matter." But, invariably, some believe and are saved.

The answer to a man's response to the gospel, to his behavior toward others and his degree of personal discipline is not in his environment or circumstance. The answer is deep within the man himself.

7

Back to the Airborne

The ring of a telephone and a Friday afternoon visit by two senior officers changed the course of my experience in Vietnam.

The call came from Chaplain (Lieutenant Colonel) Chester R. Lindsey, the 1st Air Cavalry's Division Chaplain. He told me that a chaplain from USARV (United States Army Vietnam) Headquarters was with him and wanted to see me and that they would drive over to my area immediately. Naturally, I wondered why two lieutenant colonels would be coming to see a captain, but I had little time to think about it. They were there in fifteen minutes and I was being introduced to Chaplain (Lieutenant Colonel) Thomas McGraw, the Assistant USARV Chaplain. He went right to the point.

"Chaplain Hutchens, we are in the process of reassigning some chaplains within Vietnam," he told me, "and right now we need to fill an opening with the 173d Airborne Brigade. Would you be willing to make such a move?"

My startled reply was to mumble something like "If

that's where I'm needed, then, of course, I am willing to move."

Every soldier in Vietnam knew of the crack 173d Airborne Brigade. The press had featured their exploits regularly because at that time they were practically the only unit making any significant contact with the Viet Cong. Their fame was well deserved, for they were a skillful, highly professional combat fighting force. To serve with them, I thought, would be an honor.

But how could I leave the 70th Engineers? I knew the officers and men, and they knew me. I had been with them over a year. Together we had trained for combat, sweating out the long preparation for this "restricted area in Southeast Asia." Together we had erected a fine little chapel and watched the Lord bless our program. These men were my friends. Part of myself was invested in the welfare of this unit. I would have to leave just when everything was going well. But the final decision, fortunately, was not mine to make.

Receiving my reply, Chaplain McGraw then went to my commanding officer. It was a compliment to hear him say he would release me only if ordered to do so—and he was, exactly one week later. The date for my reporting was not to be later than November 1.

In my prayers, God gave me peace about the move. I asked only for His direction, His assurance that I was in the place of divine appointment. As always, He led me—though not this time "beside the still waters."

On the morning of November 3, when the deluge of the Vietnam monsoons was beginning to give way in the South to the stifling and humid heat of the so-called "dry season," I found myself at Tan Son Nhut Airfield in Saigon with two duffel bags and a huge supply of Bibles and Christian literature. Suddenly there was a stranger at my side saluting smartly.

"All the way, sir," snapped Sp-4 Larry Chambers.

"Airborne," I replied.

That typical greeting of the airborne troops filled me with nostalgia for I had served from 1955 to 1957 as an enlisted GI with the paratroopers—the airborne infantry. My outfit had been the 511th Airborne Infantry Regiment, of the now nonexistent 11th Airborne Division. Since that experience I had been infected with the *esprit de corps* that marks the American paratrooper. Among conventional soldiers he is the professional without peer. Hearing Chambers' *gung-hu* greeting, peculiar only to airborne units, made me realize for certain I was once again with the Army's elite—the airborne infantry soldier, the paratrooper. It was good to be back.

The 173d Airborne Brigade (Separate) was organized on June 5, 1963, to fulfill the Army's need for a swift striking force in the Pacific. Based on the island of Okinawa, "keystone of the Pacific," these men were trained extensively in guerrilla operations, small unit fighting and jungle warfare. After two years of preparation and some 65,000 parachute jumps in seven countries, these men were ready on short notice to move to any area of the Pacific. Vietnam consequently became their new home.

On May 5, 1965, the 173d Airborne Brigade (Separate) became the first ground combat unit of the United States Army employed in Vietnam. Their mission was to secure vital installations in their assigned area of responsibility by vigorous patrolling and by both large- and small-scale search and destroy operations. Their base camp was located at the northern outskirts of Bien Hoa and south of the confluence of the Song Be and Dong Nai rivers. These rivers flow through and form part of the boundary of the infamous War Zone "D," which to many "Sky Soldiers" became their second home.

I was two days late for my scheduled November 1 arrival because I couldn't get a plane out of An Khe in time to report.

"Well," said Major Kamandoulos, the brigade adjutant, "glad to see you made it all right, Chaplain. We were beginning to get a little worried about you. We are glad to have you."

He invited me to sit in on the daily brigade staff meeting just convening. "It will give you a chance to meet our Brigade Commander General Williamson and some of the other men," he said.

"Fine," I replied. "Let's go."

Sitting in the rear of a room filled with some twenty-five officers, I soon sensed that a big operation was under discussion. Major Kamandoulos carefully briefed the officers on the pertinent S-1 (Adjutant) functions. An air of relaxed formality characterized the meeting, tempered with the confidence of high professionalism. Each officer made his comments brief, addressing himself to a crew-cut, white-haired gentleman sitting front row center. This had to be General Williamson, I thought. And it was.

Brigadier General Ellis W. Williamson had commanded the 173d from its organization in Okinawa to their introduction to the Vietnam conflict. Before receiving his commission in 1941 from Atlantic Christian College, General Williamson had considered vocational Christian service with the Southern Baptist Convention. In addition to training in the Command and General Staff College, the Armed Forces Staff College and the National War College, the General had attended the Graduate School of Business at Harvard and earned a Master's Degree in International

Affairs from George Washington University. His decorations include the Distinguished Service Cross, the Silver Star (4 Oak Leaf Clusters), the Legion of Merit (1 Oak Leaf Cluster), the Bronze Star (3 Oak Leaf Clusters), the Purple Heart (2 Oak Leaf Clusters), the British Distinguished Service Order and the French *Croix de guerre*. A soldier's soldier, a general's general, a man of bearing and depth of character.

He rose to conclude the meeting. "Gentlemen," he said, "we are about to practice our profession once again. Let us be cautious but not timid, aggressive but not reckless. Above all, let us make maximum use of bombs and bullets rather than bodies."

He paused, meeting the gaze of each man present. "That's all I have, gentlemen. Good luck to you."

The brigade executive officer called us to attention as General Williamson moved to the rear of the building. He paused as he passed me.

"Chaplain," he said, extending his hand. "I'm glad to have you aboard."

"Thank you, sir. I'm glad to be here."

His grasp was firm and hearty. With a smile and an added handshake, he was gone. I felt officially welcomed as a member of the 173d Airborne Brigade. Now what?

"You won't have long to wait," Brigade Chaplain (Major) Frank Vavren told me. "The 1st Battalion is going out on an operation in the morning—destination War Zone 'D.' You are the Protestant Chaplain assigned to the 1st Battalion of the 503d Airborne Infantry."

The brigade at that time had two airborne infantry battalions—the 1st and 2d Battalions of the 503d Airborne Infantry, plus a regiment of Australians attached and a battalion of artillery. The 2d Battalion had a Protestant chaplain, the Australians had their

Chaplain Hutchens holding his first service with the 173d.

The Hutchens family: Jim, Patty, Matt and Sarah.

Chaplain Hutchens leads a communion service in the battalion chapel "Where Paratroopers Pray."

Christian & Missionary Alliance mission station in a Montagnard village in Vietnam.

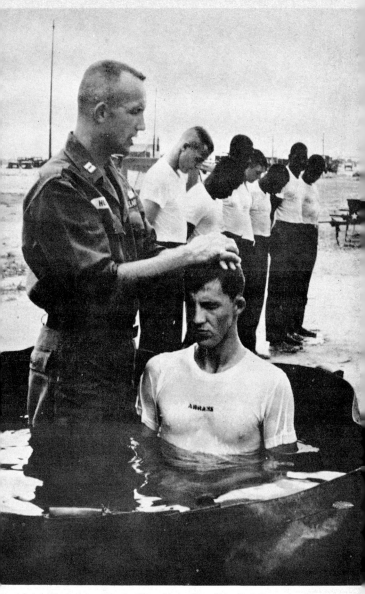

A baptismal service in Bien Hoa. Chaplain Hutchens baptizes his assistant, Stan Abrams.

A 173d helicopter assault on War Zone "D."

Chaplain Hutchens leads a memorial service for the men killed during a "search and destroy" operation near Long Phouc.

The 70th Engineer Battalion Chapel Choir.

"Where Paratroopers Pray."

Chaplain Hutchens leads a Sunday evening service in the 70th Engineer Battalion Chapel.

Jim Hutchens as an enlisted man with Chaplain Bert Hatch.

A paratrooper from 173d aboard a helicopter bound for War Zone "D."

"Dust Off"— a medical evacuation helicopter eager to leave with wounded for a field hospital.

Captain Dick Chegar, Company Commander of "Alpha" Company.

Lieutenant Pete Arnold, platoon leader par excellence.

Chaplain Hutchens with his men in War Zone "D."

Pfc. Irwin Herner, Hutchens' assistant with the 70th Engineer Battalion, holds a Vietnamese refugee.

A 173d medic gives aid to a small Vietnamese boy during a civil action program.

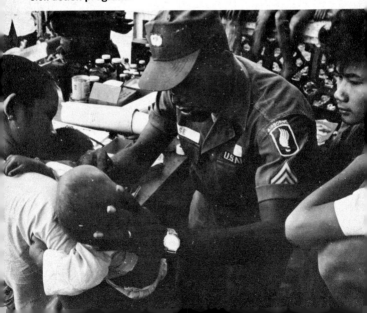

General Ellis W. Williamson visits medical center for Vietnamese villagers.

Members of the 173d and Vietnamese popular forces work jointly in building a new classroom for the Tan Trieu school.

Chaplain Hutchens holds a riverside service with the 70th Engineer Battalion.

Paratroopers pause as they search in the jungle for the enemy. Battalion Chaplain Hutchens is in the foreground.

Captain Walter Daniel and his men display a captured Communist flag in a VC tunnel network in "Ho Bo Woods."

A wounded engineer from Hill 65 receives first aid.

Chaplain Hutchens with Captain Henry Tucker ("Big Tuck"), Company Commander of "Charlie" Company, following the memorial service for the men killed on Hill 65.

Chaplain Hutchens participates in the memorial service for the men killed on Hill 65. Battalion Commander Lieutenant Colonel John Tyler is on the right

SP-6 Lawrence Joel received the Medal of Honor for his actions on Hill 65, 8 November 1965 —*U.S. Army Photo.*

The solemn notes of taps sound during memorial services for paratroopers of the 173d Airborne Brigade killed in action on Hill 65.

own chaplain, and Chaplain Vavren covered the artillery battalion and other supporting units. Chaplain (Captain) John P. McCullagh, our only Catholic chaplain at that time, rotated among the various units, making his home frequently with the 2d Battalion of the 503d. My assignment suited me fine. I was eager to get with my men.

That evening in Chaplain Vavren's tent I began putting together what I would need, finding everything available except jungle boots which I would pick up in the morning.

Well into the night Chaplain Vavren and I discussed the imminent battle and the chaplain's role in it. Then it was time to sleep.

But dawn came slowly. The longer I lay in my makeshift bunk the wider awake I became. My thoughts flew homeward to Patty and the children. Her last letter had been filled with expressions of her love. She wrote of her confidence in the Lord's protecting hand over me. She told of the experiences of Matt and Sarah, how they continually "talked to Jesus about Daddy." I longed more than ever to be with them, secure and warm with a reasonably predictable future.

In contrast to home, I began to think of tomorrow in Vietnam. Nervous energy and butterflies drove away my sleep, as it had done before the football games back home, leaving me a walking container of adrenalin by morning.

I was assigned to move out with "Charlie" Company commanded by Captain Henry Tucker, known to his men as "Big Tuck." This stalwart officer was six feet, six inches tall and weighed two hundred and twenty-five pounds—a former football end for Mississippi Southern who had married a beauty queen from "Ole Miss."

Big Tuck was a fast-talking charmer with an enviable military record. "We've had the fewest casualties of any company in the brigade since we've been here," he told me with deserved pride.

A five-hour delay held us at camp until 1:00 P.M. We passed the time making small talk, discussing football, the war, religion. Tuck knew his Bible better than most of the men. He told me at the officers' mess that day he once considered becoming a Baptist evangelist.

After lunch we walked back to Captain Tucker's tent. He was serious now, all business. It was time to move out.

The faces of the men reflected that seriousness as they loaded into the trucks for a ride to the helicopter loading pad tagged the "snake pit." There was quiet calmness, detached determination that only the combat soldier understands. Fully apprised of the pressures, fatigue, confusion, pain and death of combat, he remains remarkably steady, a model of controlled power.

These sky soldiers of the 173d had gone time after time into "Charlie's" backyard, soundly trouncing the enemy at his own game. In every previous trip, they had made contact with the Viet Cong in his homeland and this occasion was to be no different.

The November 4, 1965, maneuver was called "Operation Hump," so named because all sky soldiers who had come in with the first elements of the 173d were "over the hump," reaching the halfway mark in their assigned year of duty in Vietnam.

"Operation Hump" was destined for historic record. On November 8, the 1st Battalion 503d Airborne Infantry engaged a main-line reinforced Viet Cong regiment in defensive, dug-in position and thoroughly whipped them. When the smoke and fire of battle cleared, the tally showed the largest number of Viet Cong killed by the smallest unit in the shortest amount of time in the Vietnam war up to that time. The violent skirmish produced one Medal of Honor winner, a Distinguished Unit Citation from the President of the United States for the battalion, a number of Distinguished Service Cross nominees, and scores of Silver and Bronze Stars. The battalion had defeated decisively a determined and numerically superior enemy force despite the handicaps. The Sky Soldiers had done it once again in a most convincing manner.

Such was my initiation into the 173d and into the role of combat chaplain. The experience shaped my thinking permanently. What I believed about the sovereignty of God now became an experience. I saw that He alone is in absolute control, that He alone determines the length of a man's days on this earth, protecting and preserving without regard to the heat of circumstances.

This new awareness of God's sovereignty and power was carried into my preaching. My experience was too good not to share. Any doubts I may have had were dissolved in a dramatic display of His power. He is, indeed, "my refuge and my fortress, my God; in him will I trust."

Surely I shall never question His power again.

8

Where Paratroopers Pray

My first worship service after "Operation Hump" with the 173d was held in a beer hall at base camp. The text: Psalm 91. The words were etched deeply upon my heart. I could talk about little else, even in the unlikely sanctuary of a beer hall.

I preached also in mess halls, tents, theaters, day rooms, from the hood of a jeep, under a tree, out under the sky—wherever there was opportunity. A chaplain can always find a place for worship if he can find the men. With the 173d there was never a problem of getting the men. These troops were looking for answers to life's ultimate questions. They were eager to learn what God had to offer.

When the men discovered they had a battalion chaplain once again they began to pack the beer hall "chapel." Finally there was standing room only with men lining the walls all around.

"Chaplain, it just doesn't seem right!" one of my men exclaimed one day.

I thought I knew what he was going to say, and my guess was right.

"It just doesn't seem right for a man to worship God on Sunday morning in the same room where he was living it up the night before!"

My agreement was swift and vigorous. Although the beer hall was carefully cleaned before each Sunday service, it always retained the smell of stale beer that permeated everything—not exactly the kind of atmosphere to be preferred.

A consensus of the men indicated high approval of another place to worship. It was my move. I chose Lieutenant Jim Channon, a platoon leader in "Charlie" Company, to help me.

Jim was one of the most imaginative and creative men I have ever met. A graduate of the University of Kentucky with a degree in commercial art, Jim was a natural choice to draft the plans for our own battalion chapel.

Any military construction in the Vietnam of 1965-66 was a pioneer effort. The rapid buildup of armed forces gave the combat soldier top priority. His food, ammunition, clothing, medical supplies and other essentials came first. Anything else was considered luxury. Improvements at base camps depended completely on individual initiative, imagination and the ability to scrounge.

I furnished the list of what was needed and Jim drew up the plans. The chapel was to be functional, yet worshipful. It should seat at least one hundred and twenty-five men comfortably, built with minimum expense.

Jim's architectural improvisation was an eight-sided structure with beams overhead tied to concrete and steel anchors at each of the eight sides, joined at the top center with bolts through a steel plate. There were no interior supports. Adjacent to one side were my office and quarters, a few steps behind a blind backdrop from the pulpit-altar.

The Jim Channon pew design accommodated one hundred and twenty-five GIs. His red-tiled roof ate up the largest share of the budget. Lumber, he said, could be scrounged from the brigade engineer. The total cost: three hundred dollars.

Our contractor was Sergeant George Wortman, a veteran of World War II who had developed a building contracting business so lucrative he was able to retire in 1962. A restlessness reinforced by a great patriotic spirit spurred the sarge to reenlist for active duty. At forty-four he volunteered for jump school, made it with a breeze and was assigned to Okinawa with the 173d. Most important of all, the sergeant was a fine Christian man who loved God, His people and His work.

It would have been easy to garner the three hundred dollars from men on airborne status drawing fifty-five dollars extra each month with no place to spend their wages. I decided to call instead for a sacrificial commitment from the men by requesting their time and talents for the chapel project. I requisitioned seventy-five dollars from each company in the battalion so all could have equal share.

One hurdle remained. Would Battalion Commander Lieutenant Colonel John R. Tyler approve the plans and permit Sergeant Wortman to be the noncommissioned officer in charge of building the chapel?

"It's something the battalion has needed for a long time," he boomed. "The sooner we get started, the better!"

Lieutenant Colonel Tyler's enthusiasm didn't stop there. He became one of the most loyal supporters of the chapel program I have ever served under. Whether we were in field operations or at base camp, he was always in the services, unless completely hindered by his many responsibilities. Lieutenant Colonel Tyler's example and encouragement were major factors in the high attendance at chapel services. Rain or shine, there he was on the front row.

This sturdy Mississippian was one of the most unforgettable officers I have met. "Chaplain," this Methodist from Winona, Mississippi, once said to me, "God is the only reasonable answer to the unanswerable questions we face—the questions of the universe, man's creation and life after death." Then he added, "If Christ was not the Son of God and if His death was not sufficient to atone for sin, then there is no hope for any man."

To hear this man talk in different surroundings or on different subjects one might not guess he had these convictions. Like many other combat commanders, Tyler could charge the air blue with his adjectives and stand tall the ear of the toughest trooper if something didn't go right. He fought hard, played hard and didn't mix the two. This same intensity he poured into his worship as well. The Lord knows a man's heart and judges accordingly. Lieutenant Colonel John Tyler had the devotion and respect of every officer and GI in his battalion—mine included. With his enthusiastic approval of the chapel building, we "continued to march."

Response to my request for help to build the chapel at a prominent spot in Camp Ray, our base camp, was so overwhelming it was hard to find work for each man. Many a night I discovered GIs working by the light of a jeep or an army three-quarter-ton truck. Many a night we were lulled to sleep by the drone of a cement mixer or the staccato of hammers.

Christmas came and went, and on New Year's Day

we were ordered into the "Plain of Reeds" in Vietnam's delta country for an operation lasting from twenty to thirty days. However, Lieutenant Colonel Tyler told me during operation that he desired to have the chapel ready for a service on Sunday, February 20, 1966. That was the eve of General Williamson's departure for a new post as Assistant Commandant of the US Army Infantry School at Fort Benning, Georgia. Knowing of the general's deep religious faith, Lieutenant Colonel Tyler thought it would be appropriate to have him speak. As for the building deadline? Tyler promised, "I'll take care of that!"

At two o'clock in the morning of February 20, the last nail went into our prize battalion chapel that had inscribed over the entrance "Where Paratroopers Pray."

Our first meeting was a memorial service for Sergeant (E-6) Larry S. Pierce, the second man to receive the Medal of Honor in the Vietnam War, an honor awarded posthumously by the President of the United States to his family. The brave man was a squad leader of the Reconnaissance Platoon of the 1st Battalion 503d Airborne Infantry. During an operation near Ben Cat on September 20, 1965, he threw himself on a claymore mine, thereby saving the lives of the men in his squad. Chaplain Frank Vavren helped to carry him off the battlefield and stayed with him till he died.

My research revealed that Sergeant Pierce was an outstanding young noncommissioned officer, well trained and highly proficient. I could not determine, however, his convictions in matters of faith for these he had kept to himself. But Sergeant Pierce had revealed an overwhelming concern for those with whom he served. His brave, self-sacrificing act revealed great depth of character.

Sergeant Pierce's action was a visible display of Christ's profound statement in John 15:13: "Greater love hath no man than this, that a man lay down his life for his friends." This passage of Scripture is inscribed on the sergeant's memorial plaque outside the chapel. It was also the passage that Lieutenant Colonel Tyler quoted in his opening remarks at the dedication service. These are the cherished words of our commander, spoken in the stillness of that first Sunday morning:

"Centuries ago there was a Man who walked the dusty roads of a land far removed from us today. His life and actions produced widely diverse responses among those who knew Him. Some called Him demon-possessed; others labeled Him a wine-bibber; still others acclaimed Him as a prophet; and others called Him a king.

"You and I know Him as Jesus of Nazareth, the Son of God, the Saviour. This same Jesus was slain—but not without reason. It was because of His unlimited love for men like you and me. What is even more remarkable, we are further instructed that if we are willing to place our faith in Him, we have His guarantee of eternal life.

"Today, we come together to give honor to one who, like the Nazarene, gave his life that others might live. Sergeant Larry S. Pierce has put into practice for the world to see this principle. 'Greater love hath no man than this, that a man lay down his life for his friends.'"

Lieutenant Colonel Tyler bowed his head a moment, then returned slowly to his seat. General Williamson was absent, having been called to the Allied Military Assistance Command in Saigon by General William C. Westmoreland, so I rose and gave the benediction. Nearly every man of the battalion, regardless of his religion, remained for the worship service which followed a brief recess.

The dedication service kicked off an avalanche of activity which centered in the new chapel where the power and presence of the living God were felt in unique ways. How good it was to return from combat operations in the field to the sanctuary of Pierce Chapel, "Where Paratroopers Pray."

Our nine o'clock Sunday morning service was so well attended it became necessary to have a second service. Wednesday nights were reserved for prayer and Bible study. We later began a Tuesday "Film Night" with first-run features provided by the Army. I discovered that the film library also stocked some fine Christian films. Requesting permission from Lieutenant Colonel Tyler to show them I was told, "Drive on!"

The following Tuesday we showed a Moody Science film to a rather large audience. Many of the men came out of curiosity or for something to kill the boredom of camp.

Again I established a literature table in the chapel with books brought down from An Khe. By this time I had received even more reading materials from friends in the United States to augment my ministry. Men came in at all hours of the day, often at night, and browsed through books. Eternity will reveal, I am certain, many ways in which literature was used to lead a soldier to place his faith in the risen Christ and to encourage believers to grow up into spiritual maturity.

For me, the services were the focal point of my work. "How shall they believe in him of whom they have not heard?" I brought in heavy artillery to proclaim the unsearchable riches of Christ. Each Sunday I asked an officer or an enlisted man to assist in the service on a rotating basis: an officer one week and an enlisted man the next. This man read the opening call to worship, conducted the responsive reading and recited the closing benediction.

These personal involvements gave my men an opportunity to identify with the chapel program and the things of God. It also provided the men an opportunity to assume leadership in the spiritual area in a way not often open to a soldier. And finally, it also provided a good opportunity for the troops in the pew to see the same men who led them on the battlefield active in spiritual leadership as well.

The first man from 173d selected to lead the service was the Company Commander of Alpha Company, Captain Dick Chegar. When I was homeless before the chapel and my adjoining quarters were completed, this 1962 West Point graduate invited me to bring my gear and stay with him. We discovered we had grown up only about three blocks from each other in Kokomo, Indiana, although we hadn't met stateside—probably because I was several years older.

Dick had grown up under nominal religious influence, but his alert mind was riddled with unresolved questions about life's basic issues. He wrestled with the problems of death, of evil, of Satan as a person rather than as the absence of good. He was amazed to discover that Christ's claim to deity had not left us with an option of looking to Him as a good teacher or an example or a martyr for a worthy cause. Jesus had made claims no man can make. He claimed to be one with God, the way to God, the One who could forgive sin. If He was not what and who He claimed to be, and if He could not do what He said he could do, then He was not even a good man. Either He was not in control of His faculties, or else He was deliberately deceiving His followers. Further, if this were true,

through the ages Christianity had been guilty of per-
petrating a lie. No, the captain had to face it squarely:
Jesus was not just a good man or a good teacher. He
was God. Our choice is to believe or reject that. My
roommate always heard me out, injecting at times his
own questions and comments.

I began to pray for Dick. I asked God to work in
his life, granting him the grace to receive the Saviour
for himself. For nearly three months we talked. I
never forced an issue but rather encouraged Dick to
consider spiritual things seriously. I gave him literature to read and continued to engage him in conversation concerning the Bible and its teaching regarding
Christ.

By the middle of March, 1966, I began stressing in
my sermons the necessity for a Christian to show
openly the evidence of his faith by his life. Telling the
story of the conversion of the Ethiopian eunuch in
chapter 8 of Acts, I emphasized that the eunuch demonstrated his faith by proclaiming it publicly in baptism. Further, I said, there were undoubtedly some
present in Pierce Chapel who had never expressed
their faith in this manner and I suggested they see me
after the service or anytime thereafter. The response
was immediate and encouraging.

Some of the soldiers had inquired already about
baptism. Others didn't grasp the full significance of
the rite. Getting together with these men gave me an
opportunity not only to share the meaning of baptism
but, more important, to confront them with the need
of a personal commitment to Christ.

And then there was Captain Dick Chegar.

One evening after dinner he signaled to me as I was
leaving the officers' club and joined me for a walk to
the chapel. I sensed that something was on his mind

so I commented about the approaching baptismal service. This broke the ice.

"You know, Jim," he said, "I've been thinking a lot about what we've been discussing, especially this business of expressing what one believes. I think this is what I need to do."

"Do you mean being baptized, Dick?"

"Yes," he replied, "primarily that, I guess."

"Well, Dick," I continued, "baptism is essentially a public testimony of what you believe about Jesus Christ. Let me ask this. Do you believe Jesus Christ is the Son of God, that He died for your sins, that He rose again from the grave?"

"Yes, I do," he nodded.

"Have you made Him your own personal Saviour, Dick?" I probed

"Yes, I have," he assured me.

My heart swelled up in my chest. "I can't tell you what it means to hear you say that, Dick. Certainly the Lord has been at work in your life. I rejoice with you in your decision."

I held out my hand. "Welcome to God's family!"

It was nearly dark now as I neared the chapel but I couldn't see too well anyway for the tears. Sometimes the Lord overwhelms a man with how good He is, and that was one of those times for me. As He had promised, God had used the prayer and personal witness of one of His own. Never had I pressed Dick about his commitment to Christ. The praise for this trophy of grace is to God alone.

On Good Friday, April 8, 1966, Dick Chegar publicly professed Jesus Christ as his Lord and Saviour in baptism. The first to congratulate him was our Battalion Commander Lieutenant Colonel John Tyler. And if one had looked closely, I think he would have seen

that the colonel's eyes too were a bit misty as he
clasped Dick's hand in both of his.

The undignified death of Jesus Christ that pre-
cludes our own penalty of spiritual death is a truth
which the combat soldier can readily understand. He
sees death in nearly every encounter with the enemy.
What is more, he sees a man die in his place. This is
reality because he experiences it. It is the story of the
gospel enacted in all its bloody and violent humilia-
tion. The men on patrol with Sergeant Larry Pierce
recognized that they were allowed to live by the sac-
rifice of another and they would be eternally grateful
for it.

Finding men like Dick Chegar gave my Vietnam
experiences meaning. And when I returned to the United States I saw Dick while he was visiting friends in
the Chicago area. I asked him to accompany me to a
service in a suburban church and say a word about
those eventful days half a world away. His remarks
were fresh and genuine, uncluttered with clichés,
right from the heart. They were simple yet profound,
deeply moving to all who heard him.

9

Between Operations

War is not all combat. War is sometimes boredom and fatigue and gnawing loneliness. The successful soldier learns not only how to survive the violent engagements with his enemy but also how to conquer the long stretches of unchallenging inactivity.

The crack combat unit of the 173d Airborne Brigade attacked this enemy Inactivity with programs of civic action on behalf of the South Vietnamese. This performance above and beyond the call of military duty served well to sow seeds of a better way of life than our Vietnamese friends had ever experienced.

In our battalion it started out in a small way with trips by our surgeon and a couple of medics into villages for informal clinics to attend the sick. Then minor engineering projects began getting under way as our men dug wells; mended roads, houses and drainage systems; and improved sanitation conditions. Our big project was the erection of a school at the request of the village chief.

Although little publicized, these efforts continued throughout the war with increased emphasis as the military was made aware of the need. Civic action by GIs reached out to the sick and hungry, the homeless and orphaned, the frightened and needy in a little country that has known too much war and too little peace.

Just before leaving Vietnam I talked with Major James Anderson, our battalion executive officer, about these matters. He showed me plans to build a whole community that would be called "Rock City." The new urban development was so named after the 503d Airborne Infantry, which was nicknamed "The Rock" because of its World War II exploits on "The Rock," the island of Corregidor.

"Rock City" was to be an autonomous community providing homes for more than one hundred and fifty families. There were to be a medical dispensary, a school, a place of worship, a marketplace, a home for the chief as well as enough two-family housing units for everyone—an ambitious project which Major Anderson was determined to see finished.

We realized fully the extent of appreciation by the Vietnamese when they began bringing gifts from their fields and gardens to improve the looks of our base. They donated palm trees and banana trees, some of them planted around Pierce Chapel, to add a touch of beauty to the whole battalion area.

Just as the soldier's job is not all fighting, the chaplain's work is not all preaching and praying. He finds himself in many situations never mentioned in seminary or chaplains school.

A case in point is the "Prop Blast" initiation party planned traditionally by airborne units to welcome newly assigned officers and men. Prop blast is a term to describe that burst of air from the plane's propellers which hits a paratrooper as he jumps out. It thrusts him to the rear of the plane, tossing him about in midair like a toy soldier on a string, his arms and legs outstretched in awkward positions.

Once a man is initiated at a Prop Blast Party he need never go through it again—unless he fails the test. The party is organized much like the jump school program. The men are first formed into ranks and given a rigorous workout in physical training—push-ups, sit-ups and every kind of strenuous calisthenics imaginable. Then they are required to practice parachute landing falls by jumping off chairs, steps and tables. Finally the initiate must stand before the Prop Blast Board to answer questions. At any time during the evening, if he makes a mistake he "chug-a-lugs" a potent elixir of non-neutralized spirits. This continues throughout the whole evening until the initiates are so worn out and "well oiled" that they cannot answer anything correctly.

Since I was a chaplain and a teetotaler, as they all knew, I wondered how I should handle this phase of the rite. We had been together in some rough life-and-death episodes when we had been shot at and hit, when we had been so exhausted that we thought we couldn't move another inch. I had sweat with these men, bled with them and stood with them when decisions were made which cost them their limbs and their lives. I had prayed for these men too, and many of them had prayed with me. We had a special rapport known only to men who have endured hard times together. Still, I was their chaplain, God's representative among them, and I did not drink.

Finally I decided that I could neither withdraw from the ceremonies nor drink the elixir. I would chug-a-lug it by throwing it over my shoulder. I never had to do that, but afterward I wished that I could have, for my "elixir" was lukewarm water. Every time I made a "mistake," I had to drink a cup of warm water. I'm certain I never made as many mistakes in my life as I did that evening. For three hours I drank cup after cup of unpalatable lukewarm water.

Near the end of the party, each of us was rigged with an actual parachute and reserve chute, then made to exit from a mock-up plane door inside the Battalion Officers' Club. We had to make proper landing falls on the floor, then recover to a standing position, come to attention, salute the president of the board, sound off with our stick number (mine was the ominous number thirteen) and request permission to partake again of the Prop Blast elixir.

"Well, well, well," said Lieutenant Colonel Tyler as he rose to his feet. "Candidate Thirteen. We *are* glad to have you with us tonight!"

The men roared as he asked, "Are you glad to be with us tonight, Candidate Thirteen?"

"Sir," I replied, "I am so proud to be here I could burst!" That was more truth than poetry.

From the corners of the room I could hear some loud encouragement. "Thataway, Hutch. Stay with him!"

"Well, Candidate Thirteen, your enthusiasm is most contagious. Tell me, are you prepared to partake of the Prop Blast elixir?" he teased as he set the container before me.

When I paused someone yelled, "Go on, Hutch. You've got it made now."

I swallowed hard and replied, "Yes, sir." Then I looked at the container.

It was an old 105mm howitzer casing with two reserve parachute handles attached to the sides. The shell stood sixteen inches high, four inches wide, covered with chrome plating. Did he expect me to drink *all that*—whatever it was?

The rules stated that the contents had to be consumed in four seconds, the average time for a normal parachute to employ during a jump. I was concerned not only about the quantity but the quality of the drink before me. I had no idea what it might be. They had played my game so far; they had honored my decision not to drink—until now. If they were going to get me, this was their chance. But I had come to the point of no return so I picked up the container, telling myself that if it was stronger than cola I would throw it over my shoulder.

"Well, Candidate Thirteen," droned the Colonel, "you may partake at my command. Get ready."

I stiffened.

"Get set—"

I clasped the handles.

"Partake!"

"One thousand!" yelled the men as they began the count-down.

Cautiously I brought it to my lips as they yelled, "Two thousand!" I tasted it. More lukewarm water.

"Three thousand!"

Savagely I gulped the water like a man dying of thirst, which I certainly was not.

"Four thousand!" they yelled at last. And it was empty, *really* empty. Later I learned that a tin cup had been welded to the inside of the casing so that it held not sixteen inches of "elixir" but a cupful.

Now everyone was laughing and patting me on the back. Somebody yelled, "Good show, Hutch!" Lieutenant Colonel Tyler stuck out his hand. "Congratulations, Candidate Thirteen," he said. "Consider yourself prop-blasted." Then he turned to the men and commanded, "Three cheers for Candidate Thirteen."

"Hurrah! Hurrah! Hurrah!" they shouted, and the Prop Blast Party was over as far as I was concerned.

As I walked out of the officers' club that night Peter

Arnold fell into stride beside me. He was a young lieutenant who was new to the unit.

"I really appreciated what you did tonight, Chaplain," he said. "I know you didn't have to do that and I'm sure you probably didn't want to. But it meant a lot to me to see you there. You know, Chaplain, I'm a Christian. I guess I don't live the way I should, but I do love the Lord."

As I turned to look at him I saw tears in his eyes as he said, "Will you pray for me, Chaplain?"

"I sure will, Pete," I promised, and I did. Later I saw Pete Arnold's prayer and mine answered in a remarkable way.

An aspect of military life little publicized was the continuing program of recreation, provided even in a combat zone. Our battalion area had three softball fields which were in use every afternoon when we were at base camp. Nearly every company-size unit had volleyball nets and the game was played by rigorous "combat rules" which produced a good share of casualties.

There were movies each night, horseshoe pits and basketball hoops. Passes into Bien Hoa and even Saigon were relatively easy to obtain. The military command considered all this small recompense for men who would soon be laying their lives on the line against a vicious and relentless enemy.

And of course entertainers from the States came occasionally to perform for the troops. Bob Hope was in Bien Hoa on Christmas afternoon. His show was a big hit, as Bob Hope always is with GIs. Eddie Fisher was a favorite too, not only for his singing but because he spent hours on end talking informally with the men. Martha Raye, a trooper's trooper, scored a hit wherever she went. So did Edgar Bergen and

Charlie McCarthy who provided one of the most wholesome shows we saw in Vietnam.

All the entertainment was not as good. One young starlet was so suggestive that some of the men, none of them prudes, got disgusted and left. Afterward I heard a great deal about what happened at that particular show.

My assistant at that time was an outstanding man from a military point of view, but he had a naïve idea of Christian conduct. He had gone to the starlet's show early for a front seat. The announcer had said that when the show was finished a group of GIs would be selected from the audience to have the "privilege" of dancing with the young performer. She had arrived about forty-five minutes late and the performance had to be cut, allowing time for only one GI to dance with her. Out of the nearly five thousand men there, who should be picked but my assistant!

"Boy, Chaplain," said one sergeant jokingly, "you must be teaching your assistant something different from what you're giving us on Sunday mornings!"

I was glad he saw the humor of it. I sure didn't. I feared that six months of witness and testimony had gone down the drain that night. Right there I asked God to blot out from their memories any wrong impressions. I trust that He did. I never heard any more about the incident.

Often I am asked if I preach against immorality. It is part of a Christian minister's responsibility, in the military or out, to consider a man's conduct of life. But at the same time it is not his duty to serve as a great condemner. My first duty is to preach Jesus Christ. When a man receives Him, *then* "he is a new creature: old things are passed away; behold, all things are become new" (II Corinthians 5:17). To do away with the symptoms does not cure the disease.

The malady is "heart trouble." Only Jesus Christ can cure this. When He does, the symptoms usually disappear.

Indeed, a comrade's morality is particularly relevant to the combat soldier for, as one commander put it, "A man who will be unfaithful to his wife will be unfaithful to his men." This is a sobering thought in light of the large degree of dependency each man feels toward another man for his very survival.

I never have and never shall grow accustomed to the awesome confrontation with an armed enemy who seeks to kill. But we had come to Vietnam under orders to do a job. It was necessary to get on with it.

10

Pete Arnold

War is as close to hell as a man can get in this life. It is fear and suffering and death and earsplitting violence. But it is not a place where God cannot reach. "If I make my bed in hell," says the psalmist, "behold, thou art there" (Psalm 139:8).

Our battalion fought as often and as well as any other combat unit in Vietnam. To the chaplain this meant plenty of practice in meeting the needs of the wounded and dying on the field of battle.

Lieutenant Colonel Tyler didn't try to prevent my being with the men. "I want you there," he told me. "They need you where the casualties are."

Traditionally, the place of the battalion chaplain was at the aid station with the surgeon where he could give solace to the wounded and dying. But Vietnam is a different war. There are no front lines. When a unit moves out on a mission, the base of operations usually consists of a battalion command post set up in the center with a circle of companies surrounding it. Anything beyond that circle is "front line." There is no aid station as such, for the surgeon

and medics move with the battalion, and the helicopter swiftly evacuates combat casualties. Usually
when a unit sustains casualties, a "dust-off" (code
name for helicopter medical evacuation) is called into
the area. The Med-Evac choppers land in a hastily
constructed landing zone, pick up the casualties, then
transport them to a field hospital or mobile army surgical hospital in some safer area.

My practice was to request space for myself and
my assistant in one of the lead helicopters containing
portions of the battalion command element. Once on
the ground, if no contact had been made, I linked up
with the battalion command post until further opera-
tional orders were issued.

I tried to spend a few days with each company
when the battalion was on an operation, keeping not
too far from the company commander since his com-
munication kept him apprised of what was going on
throughout the battalion headquarters, all his platoons, the air (for air strikes) and the artillery. His
radiotelephone operator monitored the battalion fre-
quency constantly. This way I knew what was going
on in the other companies as well, enabling me to
know where help was needed. There was always the
possibility that some other company would be hit, so
I rotated from one to the other, trying always to keep
informed of trouble spots.

Before each operation I conducted a "Preoperation
Service" at the base camp. This was nearly always
well attended. From the Psalms, particularly 23, 32,
33, 34, 37 and 91, I stressed the potential for God's
protecting and preserving hand. I always explained
the claims of Christ as the only way to life that never
ends. For the unbeliever, the need was to commit
himself to Christ; for the Christian it was to offer his

life once again to God and to ask for His perfect will to be done.

As the service closed, I left the men sitting quietly in the chapel, many with their heads bowed, telling them to come to my office if they wanted to talk privately. On several occasions this was the time when men first opened their hearts to Jesus Christ.

Out in the field we had services when and where we could. I tried to schedule a service for each company at least once a week, on Sunday if possible. Occasionally a company commander or platoon leader would ask me to have "church" for his unit before they moved out.

These services in jungle and plain were memorable. Every pretense was stripped away as men faced their Creator and Redeemer. We sang hymns from a few small paperback hymnals I carried with me. It was a wonderful sound. The men sang loudly "to keep 'Charlie' awake," they said. I often wondered about "Charlie," and what he thought when he heard these men singing. These GIs meant business and in times like these they found their deepest needs met.

My thereness policy was considered by some of the men as a kind of rabbit's foot to bring them good luck. *If the chaplain is along*, they reasoned, *surely everything will turn out all right*. Sometimes it did, sometimes it didn't. Each of the company commanders asked me to accompany his unit on operations and many commanders asked me repeatedly. Since I had attended the US Army Ranger School at Fort Benning, Georgia, and had served as an enlisted airborne infantry man in the position of gunner on a 30-caliber light machine gun, I had some experience to draw on as I went on these missions.

One such mission was supposed to be a routine search-and-destroy operation near Long Phouc, some fifty-five miles northeast of Saigon. Intelligence had spotted a sizable Viet Cong force in that area. Captain Dick Chegar, Alpha Company's new commander, had set up a company-size perimeter. Then he had set his mortar platoon and one other platoon to man the perimeter.

Lieutenant Pete Arnold's platoon reported receiving heavy automatic weapons fire, so Captain Chegar decided to send out the rest of his company. Because of the likelihood of receiving casualties Captain Chegar requested that I go along.

"Well, Hutch," he said as we moved out, "let's see what's going on out there."

"OK, but shoot low," I quipped. "They may be riding Shetlands."

Cautiously we moved for about three hundred meters in the direction of Lieutenant Arnold's platoon which was still under fire. Suddenly a Viet Cong force estimated at platoon size opened up on us. Chegar put one platoon on the line and sent the other around to the right to roll up the enemy's flank. We proceeded in that fashion until the two platoons converged on an evacuated Viet Cong village. Experience had taught us that every village had to be minutely inspected so for half an hour under the guard of one platoon the other searched every foot of that hamlet.

Finally Chegar radioed Pete Arnold to pull in his security and push out in the direction of march for another hundred yards. If we made no contact with the enemy then we would pull back to our bivouac area since it was getting late in the afternoon.

Lieutenant Arnold hadn't moved more than thirty yards when the jungle suddenly opened up with enemy fire. Every man hit the ground—every man, that is, except Lieutenant Arnold.

A troop commander can do several things when he

meets the enemy. He can hold his ground and call in artillery and air strikes. He can have part of his force lay down a base of fire while the others maneuver forward. He can move one section out to attack the enemy's flank and the other to advance. He can use combinations of all these and more. Or he can do what Lieutenant Pete Arnold did.

He made a quick assessment of the situation. He said later, "I knew we could take them." He scampered about, getting his platoon in an assault skirmish line. With that he yelled to his men, "Move out—and I want to hear some noise—*loud* noise."

He got what he asked for. "Airborne, all the way!" was the frightening yell of his paratroopers, charging shoulder to shoulder, their M-16's blazing from the hip and M-60's belching hot lead as they cleared a path before them in the jungle. All this time the lieutenant was running up and down behind his platoon shouting orders, keeping them on line.

I had seen this maneuver in training and had participated in platoon assault exercises as an enlisted man, but I had never seen one carried out with such speed and precision and such disciplined enthusiasm. This is the way the book says it should be done.

When the battle was over there were only three minor wounds and they were from a claymore mine planted there before the assault.

The Viet Cong had been taken by surprise and overwhelmed by a platoon of hard-nosed paratroopers who all but worshiped the ground their lieutenant walked on. For his brilliance in battle that day, Pete Arnold received the Silver Star. There were still Viet Cong in there, and we all knew that it was our job to flush them out. As it turned out, what took place that day was only a maneuver compared to what followed.

The next morning the same task force of two platoons and the headquarters element moved out with Captain Chegar. Our objective this time was another small village about six hundred yards to the right of the one we had searched the day before. Sniper fire began when we were within sixty yards of the village, and once again Lieutenant Arnold's platoon was deployed with instructions to make a wide sweep to the left in an attempt to roll up whatever flank the enemy had. Lieutenant White, the other platoon leader, was told to send out a squad to reconnoiter the right of the village.

Arnold and his men had been gone less than ten minutes when we heard a heavy exchange of fire in that direction. Almost at once he radioed to Captain Chegar.

"Sir, we've hit a dug-in Viet Cong force. I can't tell yet how many there are. Right now we're having trouble advancing. I'm going to try to roll up the flanks. Over."

"Drive on!" Chegar responded.

The captain called back the reconnaissance squad and prepared the other platoon to move out to assist Arnold's platoon. This was easier ordered than accomplished, for as we moved forward and left we encountered the same force that was extended to the right of Arnold's position.

The air was now alive with the cacophony of small-arms fire. Lieutenant Jim Dowdy, our Artillery Forward Observer, was on the radio directing the 105mm howitzer support available to us. Bullets whined as they knocked off leaves less than three feet from the ground.

At the first outburst of fire, everyone had hit the ground. But a battle cannot be fought completely from a prone position and Captain Chegar was the first to move.

"Lieutenant White," he barked, "bring your men up on the line. Position a squad around that building!"

As the lieutenant jumped up he likewise shouted orders to his sergeants and they got the men in position. But their advance was stopped almost before it began. White's point man was hit and every time anyone advanced to get him we took more casualties.

Chegar yelled, "Hold what you've got! I'll check with Pete Arnold."

But Arnold was having the same trouble, only worse.

"We're moving forward slowly, sir," he replied, "but some of our men have been hit."

"How many?"

"Two squad leaders, I know, and some men in each of the squads. Man alive, sir," he shouted, "they've got claymores all over this place!"

After a minute Captain Chegar told him, "Pete, I'm heading for your position. I'll be coming up from your rear. Tell your men to keep a lookout for me."

"Right, sir."

"Are you ready, Hutch?" Dick asked.

"I'm right behind you," I assured him.

"Then let's make a run for it."

The captain jumped up and made for the nearest tree. Behind him was his radiotelephone operator. I was next, then my assistant and the four or five other men who made up the command element—a medic, an engineer or two and an artillery radiotelephone operator.

Keeping low and zigzagging from tree to tree, it took us approximately ten minutes to reach the men Arnold had positioned for his rear security.

"Over here, sir," they yelled. "Hurry!"

As we closed in around them one of the men said, "Captain Chegar, I'm glad to see you, sir."

"How's that?"

"Sir, Lieutenant Arnold has been hit and hit bad," came his reply.

Chegar grabbed him by the arm and demanded, "Where is he?"

"I don't know, sir. We just got word that he was hit."

From my position I could see a medic about forty yards ahead lying on his stomach giving someone intravenous fluids. I yelled to Captain Chegar, "I see a medic up ahead. I'll be there if you need me."

"OK, Hutch. See what you can find out about Pete Arnold and let me know." He flung himself back into action.

My place was with the wounded and that is where I headed. The medic had wrapped a battle dressing around the arm of a young soldier who had received a flesh wound.

"How's it going, trooper?" I asked as I crawled alongside him.

"Nothing serious, Chaplain, not near as bad as Sergeant Martinez over there," he said, pointing with his good arm to a medic hovering over a man on the ground.

Sergeant (E-6) Martinez was one of Arnold's squad leaders, a hard charger with lots of enthusiastic leadership ability. As I crawled toward him, I saw that he was motionless now and silent, except for the wheeze of his breathing. His leg was broken at the thigh by thirty-caliber machine rounds and he had a sucking chest wound. It was bad.

I thought he was unconscious, but I leaned close to his ear anyway and said, "How are you making it, Sergeant?"

Slowly he turned his head toward me and opened

his eyes. When he could see, he took hold of my arm and whispered, "I'm glad to see you, Chaplain."

It was hard for him to breathe, but he added: "I took one dead center this time; it was a claymore. Got Lieutenant Arnold too."

His grip tightened. "Say one for me, Chaplain. I need it."

I bent over to his ear and prayed, "Lord, we know that You love us, that You loved us so much that You sent Your Son to die for each one of us. We know that You are in control even here, and we know that You alone are the Giver and Taker of life. Lord, we appeal to Your grace and mercy to spare Sergeant Martinez. Heal his wounds and restore him to health and sound body. Raise him up, Lord, to glorify Your name. We ask it in the name of Jesus Christ our Saviour and Redeemer. Amen."

"Thanks, Chaplain."

Sergeant Martinez rolled back his head. It was going to be a long road back for him but God answered our prayer and let him live to travel it.

Other wounded men still mobile were crawling back. The medic had set up his own little aid station about a hundred yards behind the platoon line. Firing was still so heavy it was hard to move without drawing fire. I went from one wounded man to another, praying with some, talking with others about the Saviour, helping wherever I could. I asked each one about Lieutenant Arnold. They all knew he was hit but nobody knew where he was.

Finally a young trooper limped in with the news that he had seen the wounded man. "Yes, Chaplain," he told me, "I just passed him up there. He needs help bad. He can't walk and with this bad arm I couldn't help him."

As he ripped open his sleeve with his bayonet I saw

why he couldn't help Pete Arnold—or anybody else. His forearm looked like a dog's hind leg. A bullet had broken the bone and set the arm ajar.

"Lieutenant Arnold," he said, turning away from his own wounds and pointing with his bayonet, "is about seventy-five yards up there."

I began to crawl in the direction he pointed and saw up ahead two men crawling very slowly and laboriously toward me. A young GI was struggling to get Pete Arnold to the medic for help. As Pete lay there with his head to one side he didn't appear to be seriously hurt. But when I spoke to him and he turned to reply, I saw the tragic injuries.

As usual, Pete had positioned himself where he could execute the most control over his platoon, right in the center of their assault line. The center was hit with a series of claymores detonated electrically at the enemy's discretion by touching two wires together. Pete's head and body had been peppered with fragments from one of those mines, inflicting small wounds. In addition, there were two bad open wounds. A chunk of lead was lodged between the skin and the skull and had enlarged the temple area to the size of a golf ball. Fortunately, it wasn't bleeding. A smaller piece of lead had also become embedded in his throat making it difficult for him to breathe, much less talk. Somebody had placed a battle dressing over his throat.

The soldier who was dragging him got a grip on Pete's arm and I got under the other. Slowly we pulled him back toward the medic. He tried to say something, but I was afraid that would shorten his chance of survival.

"Don't talk, Pete," I said. "Let's get you patched up before you do any talking."

Finally, with fatigues soaked with blood and sweat

and mud, we arrived at the medic at the point of exhaustion. He quickly changed the bandage on his throat and gave him a shot of morphine to relieve his intense pain. Pete was conscious all the time. As the medic worked on him he took my hand and pulled me close.

"I'm not just talking, Chaplain. I'm praying to my God and I know He hears me."

Pete was breathing in gasps. He almost mumbled as he said, "Chaplain, do you remember what I told you the night of the Prop Blast Party?"

"Yes, Pete, I do."

Of course I remembered. Pete had told me he was a believer, that he loved the Lord.

"I know He loves me," he said. After a pause he added, "And I know He is going to take care of me."

"Why don't we have a word of prayer, Pete," I suggested, "and put your life completely in His hands."

He nodded his approval.

So I knelt beside him and began to pray there in the midst of clattering machine guns and exploding mines. Incoming artillery rounds whistled overhead at targets just beyond us. Everywhere there was sweat mingled with blood. The stench of breath made putrid and sour from erupting abdominal wounds, the stagnant smell of cavities of ripped flesh of the wounded and dying confronted this little group of maimed and halting as an army of odors. But there was, overshadowing it all, the sweet fragrance that comes only as the living God makes His presence real and alive to men. In the midst of it all, God was hovering over us. I knew it. Pete knew it, too. A hush came over the wounded men. Even the firing seemed to subside. Those who were alive and conscious bowed their heads or closed their eyes. I prayed for them all:

"Dear Father, we come in the name of Jesus Christ

our Lord. You said that when two or three gather together in Your name You are also there. We believe You are here. We know it. Knowing this, Lord, we put ourselves willingly into Your hands. Give us the grace and the courage for whatever is asked of us. We are not afraid of what man can do to us. We look to You for victory—to You, Lord, from whence comes our help. Right now we ask You to restore Pete Arnold to soundness of mind and body. Thanks be to God which giveth us the victory through our Lord Jesus Christ. Amen."

Later that day we were able to move all the dead and wounded back to a secured landing zone where they were evacuated by helicopter. Pete Arnold was taken to a Saigon hospital where it was touch and go for weeks. The fragment in his temple had hindered the flow of blood to his brain. It seemed there might be permanent brain damage.

On the day before Pete was to be returned to the States I saw him in Saigon. He was noticeably irrational at times, yet God had preserved him; and God did restore him to full recovery back home.

To those of us who were there on the battlefield where Pete Arnold was wounded it is something of a miracle that the young lieutenant is once again "present for duty." He was again honored for his valor with the Silver Star.

"He shall call upon me, and I will answer him: I will be with him in trouble; I will deliver him, and honour him" (Psalm 91:15).

Thus saith, and doeth, the Lord.

Wherever a man like Pete Arnold is found, whether general or private, every man in his unit is a better man. Our efforts in Vietnam have turned up many good and honorable men who are honest and dependable, seasoned with dignity and compassion for all human life. These become leaders whom others gladly follow. For me, I found great honor in knowing and praying for a man like Pete.

What I said that day to Pete Arnold and Sergeant Martinez and to all the wounded, and what I said to God for them, was confident and sure because of what God had already proved to me on my very first combat operation with the 173d in War Zone "D." What had been merely doctrine suddenly exploded into personal reality. The heavens thundered, the earth shook, and the voice of God was heard "to the end thou mayest know that I am the LORD in the midst of the earth" (Exodus 8:22b).

It happened on Hill 65.

11

Hill 65

Hill 65 is located in War Zone "D," a Viet Cong stronghold about fifteen miles northeast of our base camp at Bien Hoa. Southeast of the hill is the confluence of the Be and Dong Nai rivers, and north of it lies the treacherous Ho Chi Minh Trail, the Viet Cong's lifeline into South Vietnam. What began on November 5, 1965, as a routine search-and-destroy operation exploded three days later on Hill 65 into the most intense single day of fighting in Vietnam to that date.

At noon our helicopter had lifted off from the "Snake Pit" for a half-hour ride above the jungle to Hill 65 in War Zone "D."

Besides me and my assistant there were five other men in the chopper. It was far too noisy for talk; not that anyone wanted to talk. Each of us sat still, weighing the seriousness of the task we faced. One man, sitting with bowed head, crossed himself from time to time. Another had a small New Testament stuck into the band of his helmet. Occasionally he looked up at me with just a hint of a smile which told me that he too was experiencing that inexplicable peace and confidence that God gives His people when the dangers ahead look the worst. The rest of us just looked down as we skimmed the treetops.

Allied air strikes and artillery had all but pulverized our landing zone, providing some assurance of a fairly secure landing. Later we discovered that the landing zone was encircled with freshly dug foxholes and emplacements fifteen yards into the woods. The shelling had driven the Viet Cong deeper into the jungle.

On this operation I was moving with Charlie Company commanded by Captain Henry Tucker, the massive "Big Tuck" from Mississippi.

As soon as the choppers touched down we hit the ground running, avoiding the brush fires started by artillery shells and napalm. In spots, the elephant grass was as high as our heads. Captain Tucker barked orders, getting his troops assembled. Everyone had raced for the wood line. Now we came back, quickly assembled and prepared to move out.

We had landed on the north bank of the Dong Nai River. From there we pushed northward toward the Ho Chi Minh Trail.

My stint in the infantry as an enlisted man, as well as my indoctrination by the Ranger Department at Fort Benning, Georgia, made me aware of the importance of knowing precisely where I was geographically. On all operations I carried an unmarked map of the area and a compass. There is always the possibility of being cut off from one's unit, or stranded in unfriendly territory. If this happened, I wanted to be able to find my way back to our troops. As our battalion moved through the jungle, I checked our position on my map and then struck out with the rest for a walk of about a mile and a half.

The jungle canopy overhead gave some relief from the burning sun, but still we marched through steaming humidity in clothes that were drenched with sweat almost as soon as we began. Burning thirst gave our mouths a coating like chalky glue. Each man carried at least two quarts of water and some had three or four. It was imperative that fresh water be supplied every day. The cool mud of swamps and marshes was a welcome sensation to our tired, burning feet.

An added peril were the legions of leeches which found their way to any open flesh, and every low-hanging branch had its own army of biting, stinging red ants which invariably found their way down the backs of our necks if we even brushed against a tree. We could do little more than ignore these pests and press on to meet our real foe we had come to engage in battle.

Our march from landing zone to predesignated bivouac was uninterrupted. There was no sign of the enemy other than footprints and freshly dug foxholes. This was surprising because our intelligence reports had noted large-scale massing of enemy forces in the area. But so far, nothing. On November 5, 6 and 7 the battalion commander sent out platoon-size patrols, but they found no sign of the enemy.

Late Sunday afternoon Lieutenant Colonel Tyler received word from Brigade Headquarters that a large Viet Cong force had been spotted about a thousand yards west of our position. He flashed word to Big Tuck who in turn dispatched a patrol in the enemy's direction.

With only an hour and a half of daylight left, the patrol started out, planning to get as far as they could and still return before dark.

Approximately seven hundred yards west they

found fresh footprints so they knew the Viet Cong were nearby. The occasional muffled cackling of chickens, which "Charlie" carries for food, was further evidence that the deadly confrontation was only a matter of hours away.

The patrol returned at sundown to confirm the intelligence report of enemy activity around Hill 65. Then we began the long wait for daylight and the ensuing battle.

Long before sunrise everyone was up and packed, ready to head for the hill. Captain Tucker was to lead the battalion march, followed by "B" Company commanded by Captain Lowell Bittrich. Then came the battalion command post with "A" Company under the command of the very able Captain Walter Daniel as their security, to be engaged as needed. Chaplain John McCullagh, the Catholic chaplain for the brigade, was with the 1st Battalion 503d on this operation and was moving with the battalion command element to provide coverage as was needed. My place was with Charlie Company, moving at Captain Tucker's side with his second platoon, commanded by First Lieutenant Ben Waller of Chicago. The platoon was formed into three files about thirty yards apart. I was in the center file following Waller and his radiotelephone operator.

When we had advanced approximately a hundred yards beyond the spot reached by the patrol the night before, we hit pay dirt. There in the midst of the thickest jungle imaginable was a small, primitive, hastily constructed Viet Cong village.

Lieutenant Waller ordered a search of the area which proved to be abandoned—but only recently for there was warm rice on the tables and hot coals from a fire someone had tried to smother. "Charlie" had to be very near. But where? Every man suddenly became aware of his heartbeat and his rapid breathing. How would the battle go?

Quietly and quickly Lieutenant Waller assembled his men. Commands were given in an excited voice like signals in a huddle on the football field. The hunter, once again taking the form of three files of alert professionals, stalked ahead on feet like cat's paws looking for the elusive prey. Were we really better soldiers? Or did we just think so because we had been told it? Could we really whip the enemy in a toe-to-toe slug-out? We wondered.

In the safety of a base camp it's easy to talk a good fight in a bull session. It's easy because "Charlie" isn't there. But this was the real thing—*real war!* Live ammunition. Instant death. It was a far cry from television or training exercises. We were in a strange jungle where men would kill and be killed, maim and be maimed. How would they react? How would I?

I saw a razor-thin line between hero and heel, between courage and cowardice. I realized anew that, like all men, I had the capacity for either, given the right circumstances, the right mood, the right stimulus. This day, November 8, 1965, on Hill 65 in Vietnam—how would I react?

Then it happened. We had moved no more than forty yards into the jungle when the whole earth seemed to erupt furiously before our eyes. Staggered claymore mines exploded all around us. Sheets of interlocking thirty- and fifty-caliber machine gun fire rained down on us with deadly accuracy. The noise was deafening, but we could hear the piercing screams of young men whose bodies lay punctured and shattered all around us. Only seconds before they had been strong and daring. Now they lay lifeless, forever lost to this world.

It happened with nerve-shattering speed. For a few

seconds everything was a blur, then I began to see what was happening. How utterly chaotic and confusing war can be when the enemy controls the element of surprise. He was nowhere to be seen, yet he was everywhere. It was impossible to distinguish the reports of individual weapons—just one long, loud stuttering bark from "Charlie's" angry arsenal. There was no time for thinking or philosophizing. Earlier prayers would have to suffice. Our very existence was now a matter of reaction by instinct. Indecision or hesitation meant death.

What had been dense mosaic of green foliage was plowed under in an instant by a torrent of hot lead. The heavy small-arms fire had leveled a superhighway, carving out a no-man's-land right in the middle of Zone "D."

Every man left standing made a dive for what safety he might find behind a tree, or a log, or even a small mound of earth. From such precarious positions those who could, began to return fire. Only now was it possible to see what happened to our middle file. The lead man had been a Vietnamese soldier who was a dog handler. His scout dog, a huge German shepherd, was one of many used often in combat operations to smell out the enemy in the jungle. This dog's sniffer must have been out of commission for he gave no indication at all that anyone was near. When the explosions came, man and dog both hit the ground and went through the whole battle without a scratch.

Our point man, just a few paces in front of the dog handler, was killed instantly. Lieutenant Walker was hit in the right shoulder and left wrist. Right behind him, his RTO had his right thigh shattered with a fifty-caliber round. I was about five paces behind him but was not hit. Behind me an engineer had both legs broken by machine gun rounds. So it went, down the file.

The twelve men in the left file had been hit hardest because they were the closest to the enemy. In the right file, not hit as hard as the other two, half the men were either killed or wounded.

All this fury happened before eight o'clock in the morning. We had the prospect of an entire day of fighting. Only the Lord knew how that fateful day would end.

Lieutenant Waller gave the command to pull back and set up a perimeter from which we could defend ourselves. He ordered his artillery forward observer, who was wounded in the leg, to call in our position and request support ASAP (*as soon as possible*).

That accomplished, we moved back about thirty yards to the edge of the village we had searched only minutes before. My assistant and I locked arms with Lieutenant Waller's wounded RTO and dragged him back. Chambers stayed with him while I helped the medics pull back the engineer who had both thighs broken. He was soaked in sweat and his face was distorted in agony. Morphine came first, and then the intravenous fluids. The hub of our little perimeter took on the appearance of a makeshift aid station as more wounded were finding their way back—some making it on their own, others requiring help.

Suddenly the artillery was beginning to come in, our forward observer "walking" it in because the enemy was immediately in front of us. Dust danced all about us from incoming enemy rounds, and fragments from artillery severed bits of leaves from the trees above us. And then suddenly above it all came a spine-tingling screach resembling a bugle. But that couldn't be—or could it?

I looked at Sergeant White, the grizzled old warrior lying beside me.

"What in the world is that?" I asked.

With clenched teeth he answered, "That means they're going to eat us alive, if they can."

"What do you mean?"

"I mean," he said, looking me straight in the eye, "you'd better get ready, Chaplain. That's the signal for sending in the human waves. They're going to throw everything at us now."

He turned back to face the enemy. "Just like Korea," he muttered angrily as he slammed a full magazine into his M-16.

The other "old soldiers" also knew what the bugles meant. Quickly they placed our three M-60 machine guns in the direction from which the enemy would most likely come. These were reinforced with grenade launchers available to us. Only two or three riflemen were left to man the rear and the sides of our hastily devised perimeter measuring no more than twenty-five yards at its widest. The rest of the riflemen positioned themselves in line to await the enemy charge. It couldn't be long now. I could hear the frenzied screams and kill-crazy yelps of the charging Viet Cong regulars and I was scared.

There's no question: a man's theology either helps or hinders in times of trial. If it is specific, biblically sound and centered in Christ then it is a help in time of trouble. But if it is vague and ill-defined it serves as a hindrance, better forgotten.

I knew that my relationship to God was sealed forever. I knew Jesus Christ as *my* Saviour. I knew I would spend eternity in the presence of Him who loved me and gave Himself for me. I was committed to the Apostle Paul's proclamation that "to be absent from the body is to be present with the Lord," and that was gain, not loss. The grave had succumbed to the victorious risen Son of God. Death had for me lost its sting.

This was not the issue. The sting was gone, but the reality of that incessant buzzing was coming closer and closer and I didn't like the sound of it. I didn't want to die—not right then, anyhow. I wasn't ready to die. Spiritually, yes; emotionally and practically, no. One rarely is. The plans, hopes and aspirations of the future just *couldn't* end in some miserable, blood-drenched swamp ten thousand miles from home, I told myself and my Lord. My wife and children needed me.

I prayed, "Let me see them again, Lord. Let me hold the wife of my youth once again. Let me tell her how much I need her and how incomplete I am without her. Let me see Matt again. He needs me, Lord. He needs my help and guidance. He needs his dad to help him avoid the pitfalls that all but swallowed me as an adolescent. He needs someone to show him the Saviour.

"And precious little Sarah—she needs her daddy. Not just *any* daddy, but *me.*

"Oh, Lord, this can't be the end—not this way—not now!"

Then He reminded me of the words of His Son as He faced the cross: *"Not as I will but as thou wilt."*

"All right, Lord. You're in control. I place myself in Your hands. May Your will be done."

Then came peace, perfect peace and not a second too soon. Then it was eyeball-to-eyeball with the enemy and, if we lasted, hand-to-hand.

Almost at that instant our tactical air support jumped into the fight. They really packed a wallop. Napalm was dropped where it would not endanger our men. Their 20mm cannons spewed out a continu-

ous roar as they bombed and strafed the enemy. I
don't know if they could actually see the onrushing
Viet Cong charge or not. I doubt it. Still they made
direct hits on its lead elements. These strikes didn't
stop the human waves. They only redirected them to
our right.

The rest of Charlie Company had taken up a defensive posture to our right flank as had Bravo Company
on their right. The Viet Cong ran into a company and
more, ready for retaliation rather than the ragged,
chewed-up remains of a platoon. The enemy was
stopped cold, taking many casualties.

Typical of the Chinese Communist tactics employed by the North Vietnamese Regulars, they
backed off, regrouped, sounded their bugles again
and charged with renewed passion and vehemence.
This time the battle engaged Bravo Command in
hand-to-hand struggle but again the enemy was
stopped and they didn't try this again.

While the main battle raged, our little band had
fought off a number of attempts by small patrols to
break our perimeter. At the same time we were trying
to move our dead and wounded to our right rear,
placing us behind the main defensive positions set up
by Bravo and Charlie companies. My assistant and I
worked along this short evacuation route as much as
we could. I moved from man to man, trying to be sensitive to the Spirit of God as I talked and prayed with
them.

By this time the fighting had subsided a bit. One
could at least talk without shouting. Sniper fire zinged
past us and sporadic machine gun fire still made
known the presence of the enemy. Most of our men
were digging in and improving our defensive posture.
Who could tell when that weird shriek of the enemy's
bugle would sound again above the noise of the bat-

tle? Others were busy carrying in the wounded and dead, along with their weapons and possessions.

Moving among the wounded, dead and dying men I looked for faces of the men who had made up the initial left file of Lieutenant Waller's 2d Platoon. Some were there but most of them were not. They had been closest to the enemy during the initial out-burst. Later reconnaissance showed that they were practically at point-blank range. Only four men from the left file made it back from the edge of the village. All but one was seriously wounded and the fourth man had the little finger on his right hand blown off at the first joint. The other eight men were missing.

They were presumed dead, but we had to be sure. Somebody out there might be still alive and needing help. Throughout the morning during lulls in the fighting we could hear the screaming pleas of the wounded to the left and front of us.

"Help me . . . help me . . . somebody please help me!"

These gasping entreaties pierced each awesome gap of silence as the battle went on.

I approached the First Sergeant of Charlie Company, Master Sergeant Edgar Board, and told him that some of our own wounded were still out there on the left front. Without a word, Sergeant Board moved toward the area where the cries for help were sounded. He returned in about five minutes to report that of the eight men out there, all were dead but one. The sole survivor had both legs broken from machine gun rounds but had somehow managed to drag himself to cover behind a tree. There, pleading for help, he awaited his fate. Little did he know that he was being used as bait to draw others into a trap. The dead would have to be abandoned for the moment but we had to get to that wounded man.

Sergeant Board had a Vietnamese hammock that could be used as a makeshift litter to carry the wounded man out.

"I need three men," he said, placing a full magazine into his M-16.

There was no order. He was asking for volunteers. Those who went would be going forward of our own positions into that no-man's-land between friend and foe. The call for volunteers was based on a need, or more specific, the right of a man to live.

A rush of rationalization flashed through my mind at that instant. "You're the chaplain to *all* these men," I told myself. "What if you get hit or killed? Then you would be of no use to anyone. Look at the wounded and dying here. *This* is where they need you!"

But another voice said, "You've been with the wounded *here*, what about him out *there?*"

"Don't try to be a hero, Hutchens. Your job is to be a chaplain. Let *them* fight the war—and bring in the wounded. That's not your job."

"How did I get into this fix, anyway? Now I must make a decision. Lord, you're supposed to be in control. You are a sovereign God. How did I get involved in this decision?"

"That's right, Lord, You *are* sovereign. You alone control the circumstances. There *is* a purpose in it. All right, Lord, I'll go."

One of the other volunteers was a radiotelephone operator, an alert young trooper with lots of energy who was scheduled to leave for the States immediately after operation to attend the next Officer Candidate School at Fort Benning, Georgia. The other was a wisecracking, easygoing engineer who loved nothing better than a good scrap. His name was Hargrove and he was a private.

Together we moved cautiously, running, crouching

from tree to tree until we reached the wounded man. Around him were his dead buddies. Most of them had been hit in the head. It was an awful sight. Their helmets were overflowing with what resembled cauliflower mixed with mucus and blood—the remains of their brains.

We found the wounded man in excruciating pain with both legs broken. The bone of his right leg protruded through the skin of the thigh and bent backward almost at a right angle to his back.

I knelt beside him. "You're gonna be all right, buddy. We'll have you out of here in no time," I assured him.

"Thank God you're here," he sighed. He was pale, almost faint, in a state of semishock. "I thought you'd never come."

"You just sit tight and we'll get you out of here. The Lord has brought you this far. He has a purpose in preserving you."

His screams were nearly unbearable. We had to straighten his leg somewhat in order to get him on the hammock. Mercifully, he fainted.

Then, just as we had him on the hammock, each of us taking a corner and preparing to lift him up, an enemy shot rang out at close range during a brief lull. Suddenly the young officer candidate who was on his last operation in Vietnam before going home threw his hand in the air, his face wincing with pain. He turned and fell. He was dead, his spine severed at the neck. Everybody jumped to the ground, hugging it tenaciously.

Another shot, from the same place. This too found its mark as another round in the leg of the man we had come to rescue. He cried out in added pain.

The sniper fired again, his bullet creasing the middle of the engineer's back and lodging in the muscle next to his backbone.

Still we couldn't see that persistent killer. Obviously he could see us and was picking us off one at a time. Only Sergeant Board and I remained. He found cover behind a tree, trying to determine exactly where the sniper was, but the Viet Cong fired again before we located him.

Realizing that our enemy was on higher ground than we were, maybe in a tree, I knew I needed better cover. Spotting a tree close by, I rolled to my right from stomach to back and then it hit me—hot, numbing, stinging. A thirty-caliber carbine round grazed my rib cage and entered high on the inside of my right thigh. I was more surprised than hurt as I gazed into a blood-lined hole about the size of my thumb.

Behind the tree, I examined it closer. Had it broken a bone? No, I could move my leg, even put some pressure on it. I stuck my finger into the ragged tear in my trousers and ripped a bigger hole to get a better look. It was bleeding but not profusely or in spurts. No arteries or big veins had been severed.

"Are you hit, Chaplain?" yelled Sergeant Board.

"Yes, in the leg, but I think I can move on it," I said.

"Try to make it back if you can. I'll cover you."

He began to lay down a base of fire with sporadic bursts from his M-16. I scrambled over to where Hargrove was lying face down.

"Can you move?" I shouted in his ear.

"Yes, sir. I think so."

"Then let's get out of here!"

Together we crawled, hobbled and stumbled back toward our own lines. Sergeant Board was behind us with his M-16 blazing away. The sniper got off one more round, this one ripping into the sergeant's left shoulder leaving a deep, nasty flesh wound.

All four of us had been hit. One had been killed. The man we had gone out to rescue was still there. We made our way to the little aid station and told Captain Tucker what had happened. Big Tuck called to a sergeant who was bringing in the dead and wounded.

"Sergeant Broussard, take a squad and move out to the left front. We've got one wounded man out there plus a number of KIA's (killed in action). But watch it," he warned, "there's a sniper out there and he's got a dead eye."

As the afternoon dragged on, the firing continued. Most of us thought we would be evacuated sometime that day, but every approach of a Med-Evac chopper drew increased volumes of enemy fire. The engineers hastily scratched out a makeshift LZ in the heart of the jungle but it was still impossible for a helicopter to land.

The best that could be done was to have an Air Force H-43 helicopter hover at treetop level and lower a two-hundred-foot cable with a litter on it. This way we were able to get out our most critically wounded. The first man to go was the young trooper we had gone out to rescue. It was good to see him make it.

Half of Sergeant Broussard's men laid down a base of fire while the others pulled out the casualties. He suffered a couple of casualties himself, presumably from the same sniper, but everyone had been brought back—walking, wounded or dead.

During the next lull, Bravo and Charlie companies sent out patrols to try to determine the enemy's movements and intentions. Three times the Viet Cong attempted to envelope our flanks and encircle us. Three times we beat them back. On one occasion the enemy effort was directed against Charlie Company's left flank. It was nipped in the bud by an alert patrol of that company which directed artillery on the massing enemy forces.

Two other attempts were launched against the right flank of Bravo Company. Captain Lowell Bittrich reacted rapidly. With the major portion of his unit he broke the enemy's advance each time, preventing the encirclement. Each time the fighting was bitter and costly.

By afternoon my leg was beginning to stiffen as the pain increased. I could walk on it only with great difficulty. If I stood, I felt faint. But the Lord used even this as I crawled among the men. For some I read a psalm. For others, I breathed a word of prayer. With others I engaged in small talk.

My wounds helped establish a rapport with the men that would not have been possible otherwise. In every way I was one of them. Many a friendship that will never dissolve was cemented during those hours —the kind of friendship that develops only among men facing death together. Ground was gained for the Saviour that day.

By late afternoon we were still in grave danger. The battle was still hot with the enemy all around us. We had lived this far together and we knew we might all die together before the day had closed. So we fought on.

As I moved among the men I watched the senior medic of Charlie Company closely, assisting him a number of times during the morning and afternoon. His actions were nothing short of fantastic! Wounded twice in the right leg himself, he hobbled about in the thickest fighting to administer life-preserving aid to fallen comrades. He crammed battle dressings into sucking chest wounds, jabbed morphine syrettes to comfort those already drunk with pain, gave mouth-to-mouth resuscitation amid blood and vomit as he breathed life into the near dead. Every medic out there quit himself like a man, but this one was made of superior stuff. He had that indefinable quality that separates the great from the near great. Many a man on Hill 65 on November 8, 1965, can look back and say with pride that he is alive today because of the selfless gallantry of Specialist-Five Lawrence Joel. His deeds did not go unrewarded. Lieutenant Colonel Tyler, after reading a résumé of Joel's phenomenal exploits on Hill 65, upgraded the recommended decoration, and one year later President Lyndon Johnson bestowed upon him our nation's highest and most coveted award, the Medal of Honor.

When Joel was first informed that he was being recommended for the Medal of Honor he paused a moment and then said, "I sure hope I get it. That means my son can go to West Point."

Knowing Joe, I am convinced that no man is more deserving. I have talked with him about his relationship to Christ and am satisfied that he is not only an excellent soldier and a hero but that he is also a Christian. Had destiny not given him the opportunity to demonstrate the stuff of which he was made, only those closest to him would have known what a remarkable and outstanding person he really was.

What was once said of the great Joe Louis could certainly be said of Lawrence Joel: "He is a credit to his race—the human race."

It was apparent now that the remainder of the wounded and the dead could not be evacuated that day in the jungle. The sun was quickly moving downward to seal another day. In the jungle it was nearly dark. Finally the word came: "Dig in and prepare to spend the night."

Our outside perimeter was beefed up by Captain Daniel's Alpha Company that had been committed to the fight by Lieutenant Colonel Tyler as a last resort. We now had no troops in reserve. They were cutting down trees and clearing brush for a landing zone, bringing in dead and wounded, patrolling the area to determine the enemy's posture. Now all efforts would be directed toward holding what had been won at great cost. On the map it was just a series of contour lines converging on a circle. And in the center, Hill 65. But to every man there, it was much more than that.

At dusk I noticed through the gaps in the jungle canopy thunderheads forming in the darkening sky. Early in the evening they began breaking over our heads a torrent of rain. It came in driven sheets all night long, as though God were trying to cleanse the hill of all the blood and stench and death He had seen there that day.

There was not a murmur of complaint among the miserable dug-in troops. Not a groan was heard throughout the long night. It is amazing what the human mind and body can endure when they must. Men with torn, mangled bodies lay quietly as the pounding rain splashed mud on their bloody hands and faces. Patiently they waited for the dawn of a new day.

I had pulled myself to the base of a large tree, propped my back against it in a half-sitting position and there prepared to spend the night. Lieutenant Ben Waller, the platoon leader who took the initial head-on clash with the Viet Cong, crawled over with a piece of old rain-drenched cardboard from a C-ration box. We placed it over our heads. It wasn't much protection, but it did keep the water off our heads and from running down our necks.

I pulled a can of cold C-rations out of my pocket which I had crammed there as we moved out that morning—ham and lima beans. It wasn't much, but it was food. And food was strength. Lieutenant Waller came up with a couple of soggy C-ration cookies for dessert, and that was our supper.

Every man in the jungle that night relived a thousand times every moment of that day. Few slept, and those who did only napped fitfully. Now and then the familiar crack of the Viet Cong's carbines would rise above the roar of the falling rain. Periodically the impudent and unannounced explosion of a claymore mine would split our ears as "Charlie" probed our perimeter.

Despite the danger that faced us at sunrise, an assurance swept over me as the night moved slowly and painfully on.

"Do you think we'll make it out of here, Chaplain?" Lieutenant Waller asked.

"Yes, I do, Ben," I replied. "I really do."

"You know," he said, "I'm not much of a churchgoer myself, but I'll tell you one thing. I know God was with me out there today. He had to be. They were falling all around us, weren't they, Chaplain?"

I nodded.

"And yet He let us live. Why?"

Not giving me time to answer, he continued. "He's really all He claims to be, isn't He. He really *can* do what they say He can. Well, I know this for sure, Chaplain. My relationship to Him will never be the same. Not after today. You'll be seeing more of me. That's the least I can do."

I did see more of Ben Waller. He was true to his word.

So the night passed, miserable but for the incredible reality of the presence of the living God. We talked mostly about spiritual things, of the goodness of the Lord, of His purpose in preserving us, of the war, of our wives, of our children. And then once again shadows could be distinguished. Day had come. The rain had stopped.

At daybreak the air was filled again with the whirring of helicopter blades. Some were on the reconnaissance flights, others Med-Evac choppers on duty for the wounded. Some were gunships to provide security for the others. All approached Hill 65 cautiously.

A few sniper rounds zinged into their fuselages so none of them landed. Was this to be a repeat performance of yesterday afternoon? The LZ looked big enough to us. Why didn't they start the evacuation?

Finally a "Huey" (HUID helicopter) began a descent. It hovered a moment and threw out smoke grenades to identify additional trees that had to come down. Then it gingerly started down, a 250-foot straight descent through a hole in the jungle. The helicopter was being taxed far beyond its normal flying tolerance. One small slip and its rotor blades would have hit the trees.

Thank the Lord, I thought. *Somebody is breaking the ice to come on it!*

Then I caught a glimpse of our distinguished visitor —Brigadier General Ellis Williamson. I felt like shouting. There's no way of knowing how long we might have stayed out there had he not risked coming in. For this display of valor and his subsequent actions, General Williamson was later awarded the Distinguished Service Cross.

As he moved among the men, his mood was somber and unsmiling. He paused for a long time before the rows of lifeless bodies wrapped in ponchos, his thoughts known only to the Lord.

Then, lifting his head, he looked about. He raised his hand to his helmet and saluted. That done, the general moved to the LZ and began personally to direct the evacuation. The search for dead and wounded GIs was continued. Soon all were accounted for except three.

"We will not stop," the general said. "All must be accounted for."

What a wonderful directive that was, for among those last three, one was still alive.

Soon the LZ was made larger and the process of evacuation was moving swiftly. The most seriously wounded were flown out first. The general's aircraft that had lain helpless on the ground for some time took out the first load and continued in the operation until the last wounded men were removed. Sergeant Board, Lieutenant Waller and I went out on the next to last flight. By 10:00 A.M. all the wounded had been evacuated and General Williamson moved on foot with the other men as they joined with the main body of troops at a large opening in the jungle where the evacuation could be conducted with safety. That afternoon the rest of the battalion was taken out by helicopter to our base camp near Bien Hoa.

The Battle of Hill 65 had ended.

12

The Power and the Glory

"I'm getting out alive!"

Like me, every wounded man on that mighty helicopter held his breath as we started up—up—up through the funnel hacked in that wretched jungle, then sighed with inward relief as we sped along above the treetops to the 3d Surgical Hospital at base camp of the 173d Airborne Brigade.

Only in later briefings did we understand the full extent of the holocaust we had lived through. Intelligence reports indicated that a portion of the 1st Battalion (Airborne) 503d Infantry had engaged and soundly trounced a reinforced, main-line, hard-core regiment that had made an all-out effort to destroy this smaller force of Americans. It had been the largest and most full-blown engagement of any American unit in the Vietnam War up to that time. A body count showed the enemy lost four hundred and thirteen of its crack soldiers. Fewer than fifty of our men were killed and about one hundred wounded.

Newspaper accounts of the battle related the details of a Saigon press conference where newsmen interviewed a number of survivors. Platoon Sergeant Bryant, serving under Lieutenant Ben Waller in the 2d Platoon, was asked about the extent of Viet Cong casualties.

"I don't know how many they lost," he answered wryly, "but I can tell you one thing, old Charlie could hold his morning roll call in a phone booth."

In his commander's Combat Note No. 85, dated November 14, 1965, General Williamson made this entry: "Heavily engaged by overwhelming numbers, the members of the 1st Battalion (Airborne) 503d Infantry proved the superiority of the American paratrooper beyond any question of doubt. They decisively defeated a determined and numerically superior enemy force despite all handicaps. . . . Our pride in the Battalion is without bounds. Men of the 1st Battalion, I salute you."

The battalion was recommended for, and received, the Presidential Distinguished Unit Citation, the highest award that our country gives to any of its military units.

The list of men with awards, decorations and individual citations would fill many pages of this book. Specialist Joel received the Medal of Honor; Captain Tucker, Sergeant Board and Sergeant Bryant were recommended for the Distinguished Service Cross; Lieutenant Colonel Tyler and Lieutenant Ben Waller received the Silver Star. I received the Bronze Star with "V" device, as did Chaplain John McCullagh, and on it went.

The Battle of Hill 65 will be fought in the minds and memories of these men as long as they live. Most important to each soldier, regardless of any decorations, is that he lived to tell about it. The sober part is that many of his buddies did not.

The hospital at base camp had been advised in ad-

vance of the wounded arriving from Hill 65. With all
the help available, I found it easier to walk from the
chopper to the operating room than to be carried. My
leg was stiff all over now and throbbing with pain. It
hurt most when I was lying down.

First to greet me as I scooted off the aircraft was
our brigade chaplain, Chaplain Frank Vavren. With
tears in his eyes Chaplain Vavren offered a prayer of
thanksgiving for God's preserving me through the
battle.

"Jim," he said, "do you want me to notify your
wife?"

"No thanks," I replied. "I'll write and tell her the
whole story."

There to buttress my spirits was Dr. Gale Thompson who had been such a mainstay in our Bible study
aboard ship en route to Vietnam. It was good to be in
the hands of friends, but they wasted no time talking.

Ten minutes after struggling out the door of the
chopper I was on the operating table yielding to a
merciful drug which made me drift mildly into sleep.
The next thing I remember is waking up with a grog-
gy mind and a leg that was throbbing crazily. The following day things began to come back into focus and
Dr. Thompson came by with a report.

"We made two large incisions in your thigh," he
began in a professional manner. One was a ten-inch
opening on top and another about twelve inches on the
bottom. This allowed the infection to drain out, although infection set in later making another incision
for drainage necessary. A wound the size of a nickel
thus became two gaping slices needing more than
forty steel sutures to close. In addition there was a
third hole on the back side of my thigh where the bullet had been extracted.

The wound across my rib cage caused by the

sniper's bullet was superficial, requiring little attention. Recovery was going to be slower than I had anticipated. All I could do was lie there and think and pray.

Sleep seldom came. Even at night when the lights were out I failed to find relief in slumber. My leg, painful in every position, grew excruciating when left too long in any one. The emotional strain of the preceding days added to my discomfort by leaving me wracked and taut. But I could testify with Mike Coursey that those days and nights of suffering were made bearable by a revelation of the Lord Jesus Christ in ways I had never before experienced.

During those long, quiet nights the Lord's presence was so real and so close I felt all I had to do was reach out and touch Him. But in those moments I was afraid to move, afraid that the sense of His glorious presence would be gone. But He didn't leave. Often the atmosphere in that hospital ward seemed electrified with His presence. At these times I neither thought nor spoke. I merely sensed.

The divine forecast of Psalm 91 became a reality for me during those days. I meditated on it and prayed through it. I was "dwelling in the secret place," and the "shadow of the Almighty" hovered over me, permeating my thoughts. His promises were real. I had claimed them for my own. He had delivered me from the "snare of the fowler." He had guided "the arrow that flieth by day." He had satisfied me and shown me His deliverance. He alone was God and beside Him there was no other. And then He spoke again—not specifically from the Scriptures, but by an overwhelming impression: "Jim, this is just the beginning. There is more to come, but I will be with you then as I am now." What He meant He has yet to reveal.

Those were days of splendor. I was on the mount, treading on holy ground. Experiences I had read about became mine. Truths I had known and believed intellectually I now experienced. My thoughts were full of God.

On the morning of November 10, General William C. Westmoreland came through the hospital, stopping for a moment or two at each bunk. Joel was in my ward a couple of bunks down. Lieutenant Waller was there, and so were Sergeant Board and Hargrove. Across the aisle was the young soldier we had gone out to rescue—his legs in traction. The place was filled with the "remains" of Hill 65.

The general greeted each man, commending him for his efforts. He shook hands if possible and then moved on.

That afternoon Governor Otto Kerner of Illinois came through the hospital. Naturally he was interested in meeting the men from his state. While I was a native of Indiana, my wife and I both were graduates of Wheaton College in Illinois and Patty and the children were living there during my year in Vietnam. She was engaged in part-time art instruction at the college.

Governor Kerner was very cordial as he expressed a sincere concern about each man and about the entire Vietnam situation and the war we were fighting. I asked him to drop a note to my wife, if he had the opportunity. Shortly after that I received a letter from my elated wife telling me that Governor Kerner had not only written to her but had made a personal phone call to assure her that I was progressing well.

Senator John Tower of Texas was our next distinguished visitor. Then the Surgeon-General of the United States Army, Lieutenant General Heaton, came by on his tour of all medical facilities in Vietnam.

Having the dubious distinction of being the first chaplain wounded in Vietnam, I was visited by an entourage of high-ranking chaplains from the Pacific theater as well as those in Saigon. These men were a great encouragement to me, for I knew they shared the same commitment to the same Lord. I was grateful for their concern and prayers.

Archie Moore, former light-heavyweight boxing champion of the world, spent a lot of time among the hospitalized GIs. We were glad to see him, of course, and I think he enjoyed the visit as much as the men.

Reporters for various news media brought cameras and tape recorders into the wards for special news features. Several of us were taped for a CBS program shown on Thanksgiving Day in the States. We were asked to describe what we were most thankful for in that Thanksgiving season. One broadcasting company had a half-hour program on chaplains in combat. Most of the weekly news magazines had representatives there. They each interviewed with different facets of the war in mind.

One of my most pleasant surprises in the hospital came in a bundle of letters from children. A friend from college, Pat Geiser, asked her public school third-grade pupils of Kingham, Massachusetts, to write to me en masse. Here are a few of the letters:

DEAR JIM:

What is it like down in Viet Nam? Is there any chance of World War III? Do the fighting, guns, tanks hurt your ears? You know I've been wondering. I do not like war. I hope it will "STOP" soon.

> Your friend,
> CALVIN

DEAR JIM,

I hope the war will stop soon. I wander how it would be like if I was in Viet Nam. But it is to far away from Kingham. I hope it isn't bad. Your name is in the time magazine. That is nice isn't it.

Sincerely,
KAREN

DEAR JIM,

I hope you don't get killed. Have many men got killed. I hope not many. Give all men many thanks.

From
DOUG

DEAR MR. HUTCHENS,

How are you? I think you are very brave. Fighting is very hard work. I hope to become one of the green burrys. I hope we win the fight. And I hope the war stops soon.

Sincerely yours,
LOVE ALBRECHT

DEAR JIM,

I hope someday soon the war will be over. I feal very sorry for the men in Viet Nam. I would hate to be in right now. I am very glad my father is not in Viet Nam.

Yours truly,
ELLEN

DEAR JIM HUTCHENS,

I know it is not any fun in Viet Nam. I think the war is stupid. I want to know what war it is like, World War 1, 2, or 3? I can't understand why you are fighting. I am 8 years old and I am in Miss Gieser's class at South School. Why did you want to go back to fight? I want to know what kind of gun you use. You and your men must be very brave. I hope it stops soon. I know you are very busy. Thank you for reading my letter.

> Sincerely yours,
> JOSEPH

DEAR JIM,

How do you like diving from planes? I hope the war will end real soon because it's hard fighting. I hope you can come home to your family. I watch Combat Tuesday night. It's about war, too. And it is awful rough on those guys.

> Yours truly,
> BETH

A memorial service was planned for Monday, November 15, to honor those who were killed on Hill 65. I was determined to attend that service even if I had to be doped up and carried out on a litter. These were my men. I had taken a Viet Cong bullet for the privilege of being their chaplain. I was not going to forfeit that privilege now.

On that eventful day I was able to abandon my bed, struggle into my uniform with some assistance, and hobble on crutches to a jeep which took me to the battalion area where the services were to be conducted.

The battalion was already formed when I arrived. Every officer and GI stood motionless with his company in a horseshoe formation around the public address system. The sky again was dark with angry clouds. A gentle breeze across the open field played with the fluttering flags in their standards. It was a time for solemn reflection, a time to worship, a time to remember. And then the roll call began.

The adjutant, Captain Dick Chegar, read the name and rank of each man killed. Then it was my turn. On uncertain crutches I made it to the platform beside Lieutenant Colonel Tyler. My leg was throbbing violently. My voice was halting with emotion as I read the Twenty-third Psalm:

The LORD is my shepherd; I shall not want.

He maketh me to lie down in green pastures: he leadeth me beside the still waters.

He restoreth my soul; he leadeth me in the paths of righteousness for his name's sake.

Yea, though I walk through the valley of the shadow of death, I will fear no evil: for thou art with me; thy rod and thy staff they comfort me.

Thou preparest a table before me in the presence of mine enemies: thou anointest my head with oil; my cup runneth over.

Surely goodness and mercy shall follow me all the days of my life: and I will dwell in the house of the LORD for ever.

I read also the words of the Saviour in John 5:24, 28-29:

Verily, verily, I say unto you, He that heareth my word, and believeth on him that sent me,

hath everlasting life, and shall not come into con-
demnation; but is passed from death unto life.

Marvel not at this: for the hour is coming, in
the which all that are in the graves shall hear his
voice, and shall come forth; they that have done
good, unto the resurrection of life; and they that
have done evil, unto the resurrection of damna-
tion.

Then as my good knee began to wobble and beads
of sweat broke out on my forehead, I read these words
from John 11:25-26:

I am the resurrection, and the life: he that believeth in me, though he were dead, yet shall he
live: and whosoever liveth and believeth in me
shall never die.

I turned, flushed and weak, to hobble back to my
chair.

Chaplain John McCullagh, our Catholic chaplain
who had been with the Alpha Company most of the
time on Hill 65, stepped to the platform and read certain prayers for the dead as well as selected portions
from the *Collectio Rituum*—the English Ritual. Then
came Lieutenant Colonel Tyler, our battalion commander.

His words were brief. He too had suffered a great
loss. Not because he had fewer men in his command
than before Hill 65, but because he is a man who
loves life and who has great respect for the dignity of
life and personal worth of every human being. His
words did not come easy.

And then—Taps, the eerie mourning of the bugle.

As I record my reflections in print, the war in Vietnam continues. Most men see little hope of a cease-fire. There have been several "Hill 65s" since November 8, 1965—the Ia Drang Valley, Zulu Zulu, Hill 881, Con Thien, Dak To with its Hill 875, Khe Sanh and many more. The record of bravery and gallant acts continues to grow. Some die; others are decorated for bravery; yet the war goes on. To what end? Does this not tell us something?

The spiritually sensitive might well share the sentiments of the late Julia Ward Howe. In 1861, when Washington, D.C., was hard pressed by the Army of Northern Virginia under General Lee, Mrs. Howe would walk, viewing the ramparts and fortifications of the encircled city. At night she saw the sky turn flaming red from bursting artillery and mortar rounds. By day she walked among the men, mangled from massive assaults and counterassaults on impregnable parapets. And then she penned the immortal "Battle Hymn of the Republic":

> Mine eyes have seen the glory
>   of the coming of the Lord;
> He is trampling out the vintage,
>   where the grapes of wrath are stored;
> He hath loosed the fateful lightning
>   of His terrible swift sword;
> His truth is marching on.

What did Mrs. Howe see? She saw with great insight what every soldier ought to see. I saw it, as did many others, on Hill 65 and elsewhere in Vietnam. One can hardly keep from seeing it. Coming events have a way of casting their shadows before them. The wars of the ages have all pointed to it. The insatiable cry for peace demands it: *The glory of the coming of the Lord,* the Prince of peace, who alone can establish peace.

The war in Vietnam—especially Hill 65—was for me a vivid foreshadowing of the unprecedented glory and wrath of God that shall be unleashed upon a "crooked and perverse generation" at the coming of the Lord.

> Oh, be swift, my soul, to answer Him!
> Be jubilant, my feet.
> Our God is marching on.
> Glory, Glory, Hallelujah!

"Even so, come, Lord Jesus."

Epilogue

On July 27, 1966, seven days less than one year after I watched my family drive away in the early morning darkness of Kentucky, I met them again at O'Hare Field in Chicago.

But it was a different man—a better man, I think—who came off the plane and walked across the runway to where they were waiting. We had all changed. Sarah, an eighteen-month-old baby when I left, was now a beautiful, affectionate little girl. Matt was taller. The tears I remembered a year earlier now gave place to a look of inexpressible delight and pride. Patty was thinner and, like Matt, far too joyful and thankful for mere words. I was forty pounds lighter. My hair was sprinkled generously with gray. I had long scars to remind me always where I had been.

But these were superficial changes. The big difference was inside. For nearly a year I had lived and worked beside many fine men, some magnificent men. Together we had seen good men suffer and die. Together we came out to find life very precious and more purposeful and meaningful than we had ever known before. Because of the living and dying, I would never be quite the same again.

But far above all this there was another difference.

Now I *knew* by what I had witnessed that the living God still reveals Himself to men who truly seek Him. Before, I had been taught it and had read it. Now I had experienced it. God still makes Himself known. He still makes His presence felt just as surely as He did to Moses and Abraham, to Paul and to John. Now as a minister of the gospel of Jesus Christ I could stand to declare what I had seen and heard.

When I sought Him on the ship to Southeast Asia, He was there; when I asked Him for wisdom and strength to serve my men, He was there. When I cried out to Him for men who were suffering pain and death, He was there. And one day when I lay on the ground with nothing to offer but blood and pain and desperate pleas, He was there. I looked up to Him and He was there.

He was always there.

> And he said, My presence shall go with thee, and I will give thee rest (Exodus 33:14).

> Thou wilt shew me the path of life: in thy presence is fulness of joy; at thy right hand there are pleasures for evermore (Psalm 16:11).

> That which we have seen and heard declare we unto you, that ye also may have fellowship with us: and truly our fellowship is with the Father, and with his Son Jesus Christ (I John 1:3).